More Weekend Quilts

Books by Leslie Linsley

Nantucket Style

Key West Houses

Hooked Rugs

The Weekend Quilt

A Quilter's Country Christmas

Country Weekend Patchwork Quilts

First Steps in Quilting

First Steps in Stenciling

First Steps in Counted Cross-Stitch

America's Favorite Quilts

Country Decorating with Fabric Crafts

A Rainbow of Afghans

Carry-Along Crochet

Quick and Easy Knit & Crochet

Afghans to Knit & Crochet

Leslie Linsley's Christmas Ornaments and Stockings

Leslie Linsley's Night Before Christmas Craft Book

Custom Made

Making It Personal with Monograms, Initials and Names

Army / Navy Surplus: A Decorating Source

The Great Bazaar

Million Dollar Projects from the 5 & 10¢ Store

Photocrafts

New Ideas for Old Furniture

Fabulous Furniture Decorations

Decoupage: A New Look at an Old Craft

The Decoupage Workshop

Decoupage on . . . Wood, Metal, Glass

Wildcrafts

Decoupage for Young Crafters

Air Crafts: Playthings to Make & Fly

Scrimshaw: A Traditional Folk Art, a Contemporary Craft

More Weekend Quilts

19 Classic Quilts to Make with Shortcuts and Quick Techniques

Leslie Linsley

photographs by Jon Aron

St. Martin's Press
New York

Preparation and design: Nantucket Press

Project director	Robby Savonen
Illustrations	Robby Savonen
	Peter Peluso, Jr.
Photography	Jon Aron

Library of Congress Cataloging-in-Publication Data

Linsley, Leslie.
    More weekend quilts / Leslie Linsley.
       p.   cm.
    ISBN 0-312-08849-3
    1. Patchwork—Patterns. 2. Quilting. I. Title.
  TT835.L5652 1993
746.46—dc20   92–41318
                                          CIP

First Edition: April 1993
10 9 8 7 6 5 4 3 2 1

Acknowledgments

I am especially grateful to our daughter, Robby Savonen, for making sure the directions and diagrams are as clear as possible. I'd also like to thank the wonderful quilters who contributed to this book, and Avis Skinner of Nantucket, Massachusetts, for sharing the Sailboat quilt on page 76 from her collection at Vis-à-Vis. Thanks also to friends, relatives, and neighbors who allowed us to photograph in their homes.

Special thanks to VIP, Concord, and Waverly Fabrics, as well as to the Fairfield Processing Corporation, which makes Poly-Fil® quilt batting, stuffing, and pillow forms.

Quilters
Ruth Linsley
Kate McCombe
Nancy Moore
Peter Peluso, Jr.
Robby Savonen

Contents

Introduction

In 1986 my husband and partner, Jon Aron, and I introduced a group of fifteen women to the craft of quilting. None of them had ever made a quilt before, but they were intrigued when we told them, "All you need to know is how to stitch a straight line on a sewing machine." The women ranged in age from a teenager who came with her mother to a great-grandmother. Most were busy with demanding schedules that included full-time jobs, children, active sports programs, going to school, and community work. One woman was taking care of elderly parents.

None of the women had ever considered quilting, thinking it was too time-consuming for their life-styles. After only one hour of talking about quilting and showing them different designs, each was eager to try it. We then gave each of them a prepared kit containing fabric and detailed directions, including step-by-step piecing diagrams to make one of nineteen quilts we had designed. We assured them that the quilts they were about to make had all been carefully worked out using quick-and-easy methods and that there was nothing complicated about the technique. Some were skeptical, worried that we wouldn't like their finished results or that they wouldn't be able to finish the project.

My mother, Ruth Linsley, had made many quilts and, in fact, has contributed to more than a dozen of our books. Since she would also be making one of the quilts, she agreed to be the person to whom the other women would go if they had any problems. We encouraged each of them to make notes about the directions as they went along, especially if something wasn't clear enough. We wanted them to make suggestions wherever they had a thought or comment that would help others make the quilt in a more efficient way. Further, they were asked to keep track of the time spent in piecing the tops of their quilts. We wanted to be sure that each quilt, whether it was crib size or made to fit a full-size bed, could be pieced in a weekend, or approximately fourteen to sixteen hours. This did not mean they had to work feverishly over one weekend to finish, but rather that each time they picked up the work, the total hours would add up to a weekend of quilting. In this way, we could honestly say that if someone wanted to complete a project in a weekend, he or she could do so. The hand quilting, which everyone chose to do, was optional and could be done during leisure hours.

The results were overwhelmingly terrific. All the women admitted to surprising themselves. Some finished quite quickly and asked to do another. Some went on to take more quilting classes in their community, and others found more complicated patterns for other quilts. Most said they looked forward to choosing the fabrics and colors of their next projects and were dreaming about the quilts they would make. All of them said they never realized how easy it could be and how excited they were to have discovered the craft of quiltmaking.

This whole project began with one quilt. For many years Jon and I designed craft projects for *Family Circle* magazine. When quilting was becoming more popular than decoupage and macramé, we began designing quilts and patchwork pillows for the magazine. Quilting, we discovered, was very satisfying. It allowed for creative expression and the results were useful. Country style was at its peak and a quilt was the perfect accessory for creating country warmth in any room. If one wanted to give an expression of love to new parents or newlyweds, nothing could be more perfect than a quilt. Further, antique quilts were out of the closet, so to speak, as valuable American folk art for collectors. Suddenly names like Bear Claw, Log Cabin, and Ohio Star were familiar to anyone who knew anything about quilts. Quilting classes sprang up in towns across America, and people flocked to learn how to reproduce and thus keep alive the patterns originally created by our earliest settlers.

However, the biggest problem was committing to the time needed to make a quilt. Many women who wanted to quilt were simply too busy for this craft. They were dealing with the problems of juggling careers and running a household, and while many expressed a desire to quilt, there just wasn't enough time left over in the week.

It was Labor Day weekend when we hit on the idea. Jon and I were in the studio designing a quilt pattern that could be made with iron-on seam binding. The magazine often asked us to come up with innovative ideas for creating craft projects with a twist. We decided to create a quilt that could be pieced in a weekend. The quilt that we designed ended up on the cover of the magazine and they were flooded with requests for more weekend quilts. And that is how it started. We decided right then that a book of simple quilt patterns with clear step-by-step directions and drawings would be very popular. The letters we received through the magazine indicated that we could make a real contribution if we could respond accordingly.

It wasn't until we visited my mother in Florida, however, that we decided to gather a group of novices together to make the quilts that would eventually be the basis for our book *The Weekend Quilt*. By the following winter we had designed the quilts and worked out the directions complete with shortcuts and quick-and-easy techniques for ensuring success. We were convinced that anyone could make a quilt and have it all pieced in a weekend.

It was an exciting day when the first quilt arrived. It was spring on Nantucket Island, where we live. One by one they arrived as each woman finished her project, and it was like Christmas for us. As we opened each one we held our breath, hoping it would look as good as we had envisioned when designing it. Every single one was perfect! The women's notes and comments were incorporated into the directions as we worked to perfect each one for the book. By the late summer and early fall we were ready to photograph.

The quilts were lively and we wanted to express their vitality. This meant a different approach than simply showing them on beds and walls. Since we live in a place abundant with natural beauty and historic sites, we decided to show the quilts outdoors in natural settings. In this way the quilts could be part of the environment, sometimes billowing in the wind with our corn-grinding windmill in the distance, at other times hanging from a tree in front of an early 1800s house. Most of all, we wanted to present the quilts and directions in the clearest and most direct way possible.

The book was an immediate success, and because of it tens of thousands of would-be quilters have reproduced these nineteen original quilts. It has been most gratifying to receive letters from readers all over the country telling about their quilting experiences, but mostly thanking us for demystifying the craft of quiltmaking.

Jon and I went on to produce several more quilting books. Most are filled with quilting projects such as pillows, table covers, stuffed toys, and Christmas decorations and ornaments, as well as quilts and wallhangings. No other book has been quite as satisfying as *The Weekend Quilt*. It is still as popular as it was when it was first published, and a paperback version is now available.

It is almost a decade since we first came up with the idea for making a quilt in a weekend. We decided it was time for a sequel, and fortunately our editor, Barbara Anderson, at St. Martin's Press, agreed. "But the women who worked on the first book are now experts," I told her. "How can we repeat what we did before?" And then it occurred to all of us that it didn't have to be a book of quilts for novices. Quiltmaking has grown so rapidly in the past few years that we should design quilts that appeal to everyone. We decided that the quilt patterns could be a little more detailed, even more interesting than those in the first book so long as the directions were absolutely clear. The diagrams would be more detailed so anyone with a little knowledge of quiltmaking could make the quilt without even reading the directions. *More Weekend Quilts* could be even better than the first book.

We didn't have to look far for new quilters. Right here on Nantucket there are many talented and creative people. Some, we discovered, began quilting just recently and were anxious to try new designs. Kate McCombe is a new quilter whose quilts and wallhangings are sold through boutiques here on the island. She began in earnest after taking a course through a fabric shop, and while she works as a full-time bartender, she quilts every chance she gets. We photographed her Mini Irish Chain wallhanging (page 136) in a delightful guest house, the Cliff Lodge, where many of her wallhangings are appreciated by visitors to the island. Kate is especially attracted to the Amish designs, and finds these easy and satisfying to make (see page 63).

Our daughter, Robby Savonen, is the project director for our books and has been designing and making quilts for years. In fact, she is working on a book of nostalgia quilts with fabrics reminiscent of the 1920s and 1930s. She made the soft flannel crib quilt on page 90 for her new baby.

Robby's mother-in-law, Nancy Moore, has a business making custom-designed seat cushions, pillows, and other accessories for boats, as well as repairing sails. She makes quilts for her own enjoyment and we were lucky to have her on our team. She made the Schoolhouse quilt on page 142 for her son, our son-in-law, Douglas, and we think you'll enjoy reproducing it.

My mother was delighted with the prospect of making another quilt for the book, as were several of the original quiltmakers. She completed the Christmas Throw on page 107 during a visit here last summer.

Peter Peluso, Jr., is a graphic designer who, along with Robby, does the illustrations and diagrams for our books. Peter enjoys all sorts of crafting, as well as canning preserves, which he sells to friends and neighbors. His grandmother taught him to sew, and at first he made many of his own clothes. Each time he came to the studio we all oohed and aahed over his latest creation. Then he discovered quiltmaking and combined his skill with his design talents. The baby quilt on page 128 was a gift to his sister Susanne for her new baby daughter.

Once again we photographed the finished projects around the island, this time giving you a little interior flavor. One of Kate's quilts is shown in an early 1800s house in the heart of the Historic District. Nancy Moore's small quilt on page 50 suggests flying kites and open spaces so we took it to the beach and placed it in front of the Brant Point Lighthouse to include sailboats in the distance. So proud are we of our historic community, and because we appreciate its preserved beauty, we think it an appropriate setting for quilts.

The book contains a variety of small and large quilts along with some mini wallhangings. Almost all of the quilts can be enlarged or made smaller to suit your needs, and you might consider making pillows from some of the quilt blocks as well. These projects range in degree of difficulty, but all the patterns are easy to use and there are no complicated steps that require expert skills. The tops can all be pieced quickly and easily, and finishing the quilts with hand quilting should be a relaxing activity to do at your leisure. I hope you'll enjoy making the quilts as much as we did.

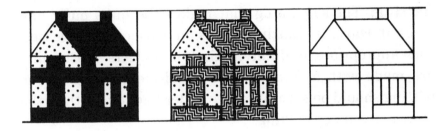

Quilting Terms

Backing: This is the fabric that backs the quilt. (See Fabric listing for types of material to use.) While I've given the exact measurement needed for the backing of each project, if you have extra backing fabric around the quilt top it should be trimmed after all quilting is complete, not before.

Basting: Long, loose stitches used to hold the top, batting, and backing together before quilting. These stitches are removed after each section is quilted or, if the quilt is large and the basting stitches don't interfere with the quilting.

Batting: The soft lining that makes the quilt puffy and gives it warmth. Batting comes in various thicknesses, each appropriate for different kinds of projects. Most quilts are made with a thin layer of Traditional Poly-Fil. The batting should be several inches wider and longer than the quilt top you are making.

Binding: The way the raw edges of fabric are finished. Many quiltmakers cut the backing slightly larger than the top piece so they can bring the extra fabric forward to finish the edges. Contrasting fabric or bias binding is also used.

Block: Geometric or symmetrical pieces of fabric sewn together to create a design. The finished blocks are sewn together to create the finished quilt top. Individual blocks are often large enough to be used for a matching pillow. If you're a beginning quilter you might enjoy making a pillow as a first project.

Borders: Fabric strips that frame the pieced design. A border can be narrow or wide, and sometimes there is more than one border around a quilt. Borders that frame quilt blocks are called sashing and are sometimes made from one of the fabrics or from a contrasting fabric. Borders are often used to enlarge a quilt top so that it extends over the sides of the mattress.

Patchwork: Fabric pieces sewn together to create an

entire design. Sometimes the shapes form a geometric block. The blocks are then sewn together to make up the completed quilt top.

Piecing: Joining patchwork pieces together to form a design on the block.

Quilting: Stitching together two layers of fabric with a layer of batting between them.

Quilting patterns: The lines or markings on the fabric that make up the design. Small hand or machine stitches are made along these lines, which might be straight, curved, or made up of elaborate curlicue patterns. Small quilting stitches can also follow the seam lines where pieces of fabric are joined. Or a quilting pattern can be created by stitching a grid or diamonds over the entire quilt.

Sashing or strips: The narrow pieces of fabric used to frame the individual blocks and join them together. They are often used in a contrasting color.

Setting: Joining the quilt blocks to form the finished top of the quilt.

Top: This is the top layer of fabric with the right side showing. Patchwork or appliquéd pieces create the top fabric.

Materials for Quiltmaking

Cutting board: This is a handy item for quick measuring and cutting methods you'll use for making quilts. It is available in fabric stores or from mail-order sources.

Fabric: You can never have too many different fabric patterns when designing a quilting project. I always seem to need ten times more variety to choose from than I think I will. Fabric is the quilter's main concern: what kind, how much to buy, and what colors or prints will work together.

Most quilters prefer 100% cotton, and most fabric is 45 inches wide with selvage. All the fabric you choose for a quilting project should be of the same weight and should be washed before it is used. This removes any sizing in the fabric and allows for shrinkage before making the project. Sometimes cotton fabric fades slightly. This produces a worn,old look that is desirable in the world of quiltmaking.

When collecting a variety of fabric prints for your quilting projects, it's a good idea to have a selection of lights and darks. The colors and patterns of the fabric will greatly affect the design. Calico has always been used for quilting projects. The small, overall prints can be used effectively together, and there is a wide variety of colors to choose from. Pretty floral prints are lovely to use with alternating solid colors that match the colors in the prints.

The backing fabric for a quilt can be a sheet, muslin, or one of the fabrics used for the patchwork on the top. It, too, should be 100% cotton, and a light color is generally thought to be better than dark (a dark color might show through the thin batting and light fabric in the quilt top). Unlike 45-inch-wide fabric, a sheet is wide enough to cover the back of any size quilt without piecing.

Iron: It's impossible to work on any quilting project without having an iron right right next to the sewing machine. After each stitching direction, you will be instructed to press the fabric. If you are doing patchwork, it's handy to pad a stool or chair with a piece of batting and place it next to you by the sewing machine. As you piece the fabric, you can iron the seams without getting up. Use a steam setting.

Marking pen: Sometimes a pattern or design has to be traced from the book and transferred to the fabric. When you want an overall quilting design, you'll need lines to follow. Water-soluble marking pens made specifically for marking your quilting lines on the fabric can be found in fabric shops. Once you've finished quilting, the pen marks can be removed with a plant mister or damp sponge. Simply pat over the lines and they disappear.

Needles: All the projects in this book are pieced on a sewing machine. The quilting can be done by hand or on the machine, but hand quilting looks best. If the batting is extra-loft, it will not go through the machine and the quilting must be done by hand. Many quilters use this thick batting for tied quilts. However, most quilts are made with a traditional batting. To quilt you'll need #7 or #8 sharps, which are the most common size needles used for hand quilting. They are often called "betweens."

Rotary cutter: This tool looks like a pizza cutter and allows you to cut several layers of fabric at once or long strips of fabric for strip piecing. It is more accurate than scissors.

Ruler and yardstick: You can't work without them. A metal ruler can be used as a straightedge for the most accurate cutting. Use the yardstick for cutting lengths of fabric where you must mark and cut at least 36 inches at one time.

The width of the yardstick makes it perfect for marking a grid pattern for quilting. You simply draw the first line, then flip the yardstick over and continue to mark lines without ever removing the yardstick from the fabric. You will have a perfect 1-inch grid.

Scissors: You'll need good scissors for cutting your fabric. To keep them at their best, try not to use these scissors to cut anything but fabric—cutting paper with scissors will ruin them. Invest in a pair of small, pointed scissors for snipping threads as you stitch and quilt.

Straight pins: Use extralong 1¾-inch sharp pins.

Template: A rigid, full-size pattern that is used to trace design elements. It can be cut from cardboard, manila, oaktag (used for file folders), plastic, acetate, or sandpaper. Acetate, which is transparent and produces clean, crisp edges, should be used for pattern pieces when a repeat design is required. Sandpaper doesn't slip when placed facedown on the fabric. If you're cutting one design, simply use the paper pattern pinned to the fabric as a cutting guide.

Thimble: Most quilters can't live without one. I find it difficult to quilt with a thimble on my finger. I keep it handy for pushing the needle through the fabric, but I keep taking it off and putting it on, which is most awkward. However, to avoid pricking your finger over and over it's a must, but be sure to get the right size.

Thread: Match the thread to the color of the fabric. Cotton-blend thread is best for all quilting and piecing.

Quilting Techniques

Estimating fabric yardage

The fabric used for all of those projects is 45 inches wide. All measurements are figured with a ¼-inch seam allowance unless otherwise specified.

Every project lists the exact amount of material needed for each color, and all the quilt projects are made to fit standard bed sizes, which are given with each project. However, you may want to be sure that a specific quilt will fit your special needs, or you might want to change the size specified to something larger or smaller. It's easy to figure what size will best fit your bed.

When estimating yardage for a bed quilt, measure your bed fully made. This means with bed pad, sheets, and blankets over the mattress. Measure the length, width, and depth, including the box spring. Decide if you want a slight overhang, an overhang to the top of a dust ruffle, or a drop to the floor, and whether or not the quilt will extend up and over the pillows. If a quilt size for any project isn't the right size for your bed, it can be changed by adding to, or subtracting from, the border measurements. This shouldn't change the fabric design.

Laying out patterns

To get the best use of your fabric, plan a layout of the pattern pieces on paper before cutting the fabric. I have given the dimensions for the largest pieces first for each project. The border pieces, for example, look best when they are not pieced, but rather cut as one long strip. The backing piece is usually cut as one piece if the project is less than 45 inches wide. However, since most quilts are wider, the backing must be pieced. If you plan the best layout on the fabric you will avoid more piecing than is necessary.

Piecing the backing

You may have to piece panels together for the back of a quilt, tablecloth, or wallhanging in order to get the correct size. Use the full width of fabric (usually 45 inches) cut to the appropriate length. Cut another piece the same size. Then cut the second strip of fabric in half lengthwise so that you have two narrow strips of the same size. Join one of these matching panels to each long-sided edge of the large center panel to avoid a seam down the middle of the quilt backing. Press seams open. If you use a bed sheet the same size as the quilt top, you will have a solid backing that doesn't require piecing.

Enlarging designs

Most patterns and designs are shown full size, but some are too large to fit on a page. In this case, the designs are shown on a grid for easy enlargement. Each square on the grid equals 1 inch. This means that you will transfer or copy the design onto graph paper marked with 1-inch squares. Begin by counting the number of squares on the pattern in the book. Number them horizontally and again vertically. Count the number of squares on your larger graph and number them in the same way. Copy the design onto your grid one square at a time.

Transferring a design

First, trace the pattern pieces or quilting designs from the book. Place a piece of dressmaker's tracing (carbon) paper on the right side of the fabric with the carbon side down and the tracing paper on top. Go over all pattern lines with a tracing wheel or ballpoint pen to transfer the design. Remove the carbon and tracing paper.

Making a template

If you use oaktag or cardboard for your template material you'll have to transfer the pattern to the template material by first tracing the design. Place the tracing facedown on the cardboard and, using a pen or pencil, rub over each traced line. The outline will be transferred to the cardboard. Remove the tracing and go over the lines with a ballpoint pen to make them legible. Cut out the design outline from the cardboard. If using acetate, simply tape it over the traced design and cut out the exact shape.

There are several advantages to using acetate for your template material. It can be used many times without losing its sharp edges, and since it's clear you can trace a pattern piece directly onto it. Further, you can see through it when placing it on your fabric and so can position it where you want it. If you are using a floral print, for example, you might want to center a flower in the middle of the template piece.

Determine which fabric will be used for each template. Place the templates at least ½ inch apart to allow for the ¼-inch seam allowance you must add when cutting out each piece. You may even want to allow for ⅜-inch seams for turning of the edges. This will be determined by the thickness of the fabric and whether or not the design has points, curves, and so on. Try both space allowances to see which works best for you. If the pattern is given with seam allowance, cut directly on tracing lines.

Consider the grain of the fabric and the direction of the print when placing your templates.

Sewing points

Many traditional quilt patterns are created from triangles, diamonds, and similar shapes. The points present a challenge and require special care.

When stitching two such pieces together, sew along the stitch line, but do not sew into the seam allowance at each point. It helps to mark the finished points with a pin so that you can begin and end your seams at these marks.

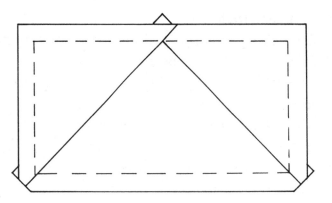

Sewing curves

Before turning a curved appliqué piece, stay-stitch along the seam line, then clip or notch evenly spaced cuts along the edge in the seam allowance (clip all inward curves and notch all outward curves). When the fabric is turned under, it will lie flat.

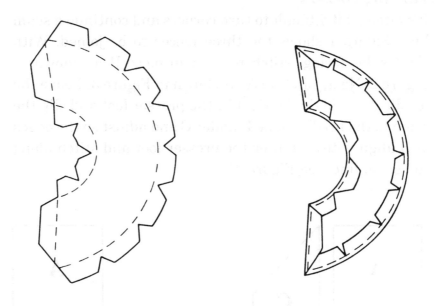

Sewing inside corner edges

Place a pin across the point of the stitches and clip up to the stitches in the seam allowance in order to turn the fabric under.

Sewing outside corner edges

Once you've stitched around a corner, clip off half the seam allowance across the point. Turn fabric back, press seams open, and trim excess fabric away.

Mitering corners

Most borders butt at the corners, but a mitered corner is another option. This means that the ends of the borders are joined with a diagonal seam at a 45 degree angle. To do this, position one border over the other at one corner on the wrong side of the quilt. Draw a diagonal line from the outside corner to the inside corner where the borders meet.

Reverse positions of the border strips (bottom strip now on top), and draw a line from the outside corner to the inside corner as you did before. With right sides facing, match the two pencil lines and stitch along this line. Cut away the excess triangular shapes and press seams to one side. Repeat on all 4 corners of the quilt.

Turning corners

It's often a bit difficult to turn corners and continue a seam line. Figure 1 shows the three pieces to be joined. With right sides facing, stitch piece A to piece B as shown in Figure 2. Next, join C to A, as shown in Figure 3. Leave the needle down in the fabric. Lift the presser foot and clip the seam to the needle. Slide B under C and adjust so the edges of B align with C. Lower the presser foot and stitch along the seam line (see Figure 4).

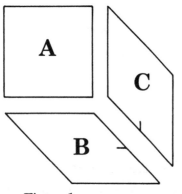

Figure 1

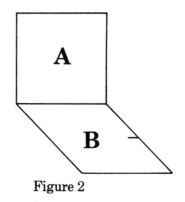

Figure 2

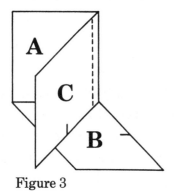

Figure 3

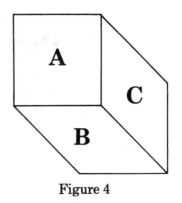

Figure 4

What is quilting?

Quilting is sewing layers of fabric and batting together to produce a padded fabric held together by even, straight, and small stitches. The quilting process, generally the finishing step in a patchwork project, is what makes the project interesting and gives it a textured look.

Basting

Before quilting, you will have to baste the quilt top, batting, and backing together. To avoid a lump of filler at any point, begin at the center of the top and baste outward with long, loose stitches to create a sunburst pattern. There should be about 6 inches between the basted lines at the edges of the quilt. Baste from the top only. These stitches will be cut away as you do your quilting. Some quilters simply pin the fabrics together before quilting, but it isn't always recommended. I feel more confident when the fabric is basted.

Hand quilting

Thread your needle with a length of approximately 18 to 20 inches and make a small knot with a 1-inch tail beyond it. Bring the needle up through the back to the front of the quilt top where the first line of quilting will begin and give the knotted end a good tug to pull it through the backing fabric into the batting. Take small running stitches. Follow your premarked quilting pattern or stitch ¼ inch away from each side of all seam lines. Do not stitch into the ¼-inch seam allowance around the outside edge of the quilt.

Machine quilting

This quicker way to create a quilted look does not have the same rich look of authentic early quilting that hand stitching does. It is best to machine quilt when the batting isn't too thick.

When machine quilting, set the stitch length control at approximately six stitches to the inch so the stitching looks like hand stitching. Taking this precaution will assure that the absence of hand stitching doesn't detract from the design.

Outlining

This is the method of quilting along the patchwork seams. In this way, each design element is pronounced and the fabric layers are secured.

Overall quilting

When you want to fill large areas of the background with quilting, choose a simple design. The background quilting should not interfere with the patchwork or appliqué elements.

To ensure accurate spacing, make grid patterns of squares or diamond shapes with a yardstick or masking tape. For a quick-and-easy method, lay a yardstick diagonally across the fabric and mark the material with a marking pen. Without removing the yardstick, turn it over and mark along the edge once again. Continue across the fabric to the opposite edge. You will have perfect 1-inch spaces between each line. Lay the yardstick across the fabric at the corner opposite where you began and repeat the process to create 1-inch grid across the top of the fabric. Stitch along these lines.

Tye quilting

An alternative to hand quilting is tying, in order to hold the backing, batting, and quilt top together at evenly spaced intervals in the center of blocks and the corners where blocks intersect. This is usually done with embroidery floss in the following way: Thread the needle with a length of floss approximately 10–12 inches, but do not knot the end. Insert the needle through the top of the quilt through all 3 layers and back up again close to where you inserted the needle. Tie the floss in a knot and cut the ends to approximately 1½ inches.

Quick-and-Easy Methods

Strip piecing

This is the method by which you sew strips of different fabrics together and cut them into units that are arranged to make up the entire quilt top. Rather than cutting and sewing individual squares together over and over again, two or more strips of fabric are sewn together and then cut into segments that are of the exact same dimensions. These units are then arranged and stitched together in different positions to form the quilt pattern. We used this method for making many of the quilts in the book. So if a quilt looks particularly difficult to make, involving the piecing of lots of tiny squares, read through the directions. You may find it's not so difficult to make after all.

Binding a quilt

When a quilt is finished the edges are bound in place with a narrow border of binding all around. Some quilters like to use the backing to bind the edges and often choose one of the fabrics from the pieced top for this purpose. To create a binding and narrow border all around the quilt you will cut the backing piece at least 1 inch larger than the finished top all around. Once the quilting is complete, turn the raw edges of the backing forward ¼ inch and press. Then turn this fabric forward to cover the raw edges of the quilt top and press. Pin in place and hand or machine stitch all around.

Purchased binding is made from bias strips of fabric sewn together. You will find packages in a variety of colors in most fabric shops. Several seams will be seen at various intervals along the binding but this is acceptable. It's not always easy to match exactly the color of purchased binding to those in your fabrics. Some quilters make their own bias binding by cutting strips of fabric to match one of the fabrics in the quilt top and stitching them together to create the length of binding needed.

Sewing small squares together

When making a patchwork fabric from small squares, approximately 1 to 1½ inches, there's an easy method for stitching them together. With right sides facing, pin individual sets of two squares each together. Stitch along one side edge but do not cut the thread when you reach the end. Simply run the machine for two or three more stitches and then feed the next set of squares through. Continue to stitch all the sets of squares in this way so you have a string of patches connected by the threads between. When you have enough for the project, cut the strings between the squares to separate them. Open each set of squares and press.

Right triangles

There is a quick-and-easy way to join light and dark triangles to create squares of any size. Once you've determined the size of your finished unit, add 1 inch to it. For example, if you want to create 2-inch squares, mark off 3-inch squares on the wrong side of the light fabric. Next, draw diagonal lines through each square as shown in Figure 1. With right sides facing and raw edges aligned, pin the marked light fabric to the same size dark fabric. Stitch a ¼-inch seam on each side of the drawn diagonal lines as shown in Figure 2.

Cut on all solid lines to get the individual squares of light and dark, or contrasting fabric triangles. Press to one side.

Figure 1

Figure 2

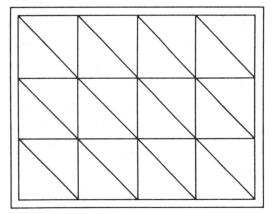

26

Gallery of Quilts

Baby Bow Ties

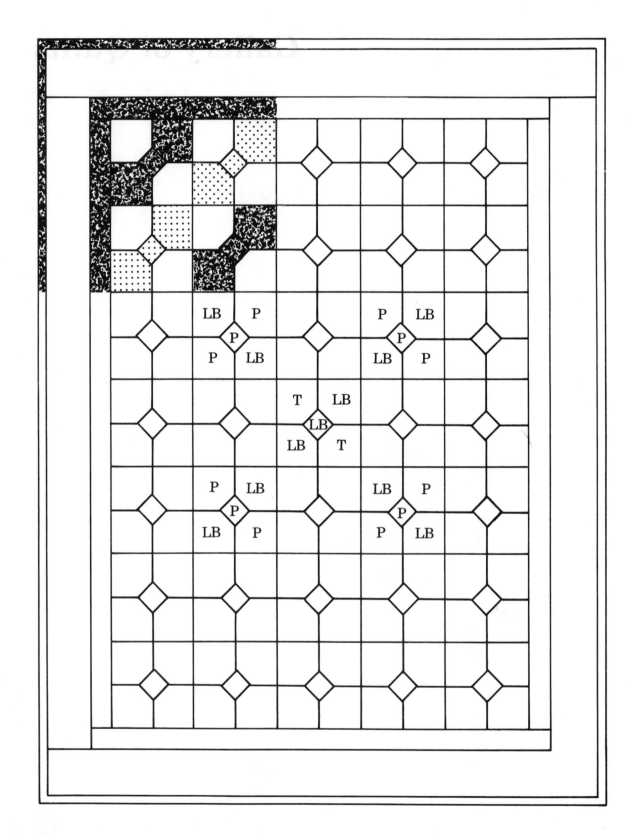

Make a crib-size quilt with the Bow Tie pattern in the colors of your choice. You can even use scraps of fabric to make a colorful Bow Tie quilt. The finished size is 31 × 40 inches.

Materials
(all fabric is 45 inches wide)
small amount tan calico fabric
⅛ yard pink calico fabric
⅛ yard light blue calico fabric
¼ yard light brown calico fabric
1 yard yellow calico fabric
1½ yards royal blue calico fabric
quilt batting 31 × 40 inches
tracing paper
cardboard

Directions
Note: All measurements include a ¼-inch seam allowance. Trace patterns A and B and transfer to cardboard for templates (see page 19). Cut out.

Cut the following
from tan calico
     A—2
from pink calico
     A—8
     B—4
from light blue calico
     A—10
     B—1
from light brown calico
     A—24
     B—12
from yellow calico

LB = Light Blue
P = Pink
T = Tan

2 strips, each 3¼ × 34 inches (side borders)

2 strips, each 3¼ × 30 inches (top and bottom borders)

A—60

from royal blue calico

1 piece 36 × 45 inches (backing)

2 strips, each 1½ × 32 inches (side borders)

2 strips, each 1½ × 25 inches (top and bottom borders)

A—36

B—18

To make blocks

Refer to Figure 1a.

1. With right sides facing, join the short edge of a yellow A piece to a side edge of a blue B piece. Repeat on the opposite side of the blue piece with another yellow A piece as shown.

2. Press seams to one side.

3. Refer to Figure 1b. With right sides facing, join a blue A piece to each of the remaining 2 sides of the blue B piece and to the yellow A pieces as shown, to complete the block.

4. Press seams to one side. Make 18 blocks in this way.

5. Using 2 yellow A pieces, 2 light brown A pieces, and 1 light brown B piece, repeat steps 1 through 4. Make 12 blocks using these colors.

6. Using 2 light blue A pieces, 2 pink A pieces, and 1 pink B piece, repeat steps 1 through 4. Make 4 blocks using these colors.

7. Using 2 tan A pieces, 2 light blue A pieces, and 1 light blue B piece, repeat steps 1 through 4.

8. Press seams to one side.

To make rows

1. Refer to Figure 2 and arrange blocks into 7 rows of 5 blocks each as shown in Figure 4.

2. With right sides facing, join all 5 blocks in each row.

3. Press seams to one side.

Figure 1a

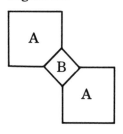

Figure 1b

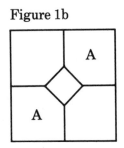

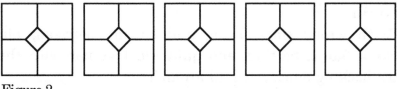

Figure 2

To join rows

Refer to Figure 3.

1. With right sides facing, join the bottom edge of the top row to the top edge of the second row.

2. Press seams to one side.

3. Continue to join all 7 rows in this way.

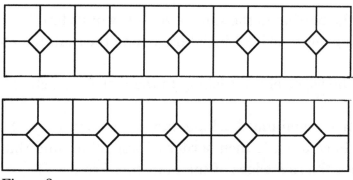

Figure 3

To join borders

1. With right sides facing, join a long, blue border strip to one side edge of the quilt top. Press seam to one side.

2. Repeat with the remaining long blue border strip on the opposite side of the quilt top.

3. Next, with right sides facing, join a short blue border strip to the top edge of the quilt top. Press seam to one side.

4. Repeat with the remaining blue strip on the bottom edge of the quilt top.

5. With right sides facing, join the longer yellow border strips to each side edge of the quilt top. Press seams to one side.

6. Next, join the remaining yellow border strips to the top and bottom edges of the quilt top.

7. Press seams to one side.

To quilt

1. With wrong sides facing and batting between, pin backing fabric, batting, and quilt top together with the extra backing fabric even all around.

2. Beginning at the center and working outward in a sunburst pattern, take long, loose, basting stitches through all three layers.

3. Using small running stitches, quilt ¼ inch from each side of all seam lines, stopping short of the seam allowance around the outside of the quilt.

To finish

1. When all quilting is complete, remove the basting stitches.

2. Trim the batting to the same size as the quilt top. Trim the backing fabric so it's 1 inch larger than the quilt top all around.

3. Turn the edges of the backing to the inside ¼ inch and press.

4. Fold the remaining backing fabric forward over the quilt top to create a ½-inch border of blue all around that will encase the raw edges of the quilt top. Press.

5. Pin the border to the quilt top and slipstitch all around to finish.

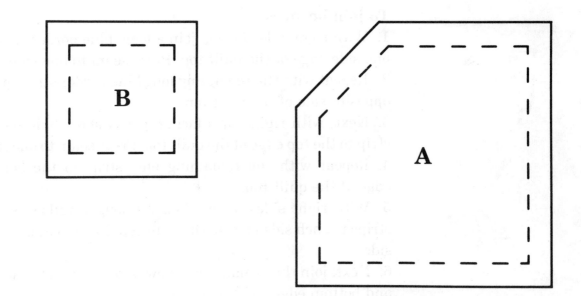

Lightning Streaks

Yellow and orange calico prints are used to create an exciting pattern that looks like streaks of lightning. Some quilters might like to interpret this pattern with light blue on a dark blue background to look like streaks across the sky. The finished quilt is 69 × 89 inches and was made by Nancy Moore.

Materials
(all fabric is 45 inches wide)
2½ yards orange calico
4 yards yellow calico
4 yards backing fabric (solid yellow used here)
quilt batting 70 × 90 inches
tracing paper
cardboard

Directions
Note: All measurements include a ¼-inch seam allowance.

Trace pattern A and transfer to cardboard to make a template (see page 19). Cut out.

Cut the following
from orange calico

  1 piece 42 × 61 inches (for use in quick-and-easy triangle method)

  11 strips, each 2½ × 45 inches (for use in strip piecing)

from yellow calico (cut borders first)

  borders—2 strips, each 5 × 80½ inches

    2 strips, each 5 × 69½ inches

    11 strips, each 2½ × 45 inches (cut 10 vertically and 1 horizontally for use in strip piecing)

  1 piece 42 × 61 inches (for use in quick-and-easy triangle method)

  A—48

Quick-and-easy triangle method
Refer to page 26.
1. On the wrong side of the yellow piece 42 × 61 inches, measure and mark 96 squares, each 4⅞ × 4⅞ inches, with

8 across and 12 down. Draw a line diagonally through all squares.

2. With right sides facing, pin the marked yellow piece to the matched orange calico piece 42 × 61 inches.

3. Stitch ¼ inch from each side of all diagonal lines.

4. Cut on all solid lines. You will have 192 squares, each made up of an orange and a yellow triangle, as shown in Figure 1a.

5. Press seams to one side.

Figure 1a

Strip piecing method

Refer to page 25.

1. With right sides facing, join a yellow strip 2½ × 45 inches to an orange strip 2½ × 45 inches along one long edge.

2. Press seam to one side. Make 11 pairs of strips in this way.

3. Next, measure and mark off 2½-inch sections across each pair of strips. Cut off each section so you have a total of 192 pieced rectangles as shown in Figure 1b.

Figure 1b

Figure 2a

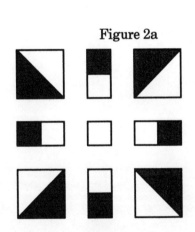

To assemble blocks

Refer to Figure 2a.

1. Using 4 pieced squares made as shown in Figure 1a, 4 pieced rectangles made as shown in Figure 1b, and 1 A piece, arrange into 3 rows as shown in Figure 2a.

2. With right sides facing, join the pieced square to the pieced rectangle along the right side edge. Next join this to another pieced square to form the top row as shown.

3. Press seams to one side.

4. Next, join the pieced rectangle to the yellow A square and then to another pieced rectangle to form the middle row.

5. Press seams to one side.

6. Repeat step 2 to make the bottom row.

7. With right sides facing and seams aligned, join the top row to the middle row and then the middle row to the bottom row to complete the block as shown in Figure 2b.

8. Press seams to one side. Make 48 blocks in this way.

Figure 2b

To make rows

Refer to Figure 3.

1. With right sides facing, join 2 blocks along one side edge.
2. Press seams to one side.
3. Continue to join 6 blocks in this way to make a row.
4. Make 8 rows of 6 blocks each.

Figure 3

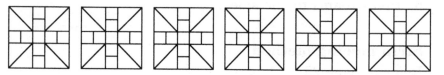

To join rows

Refer to Figure 4.

1. With right sides facing and seams aligned, join the bottom edge of the first row to the top edge of the second row.
2. Press seams to one side.
3. Continue to join all 8 rows in this way to make the quilt top.

Figure 4

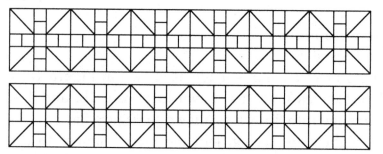

To join borders

1. With right sides facing, join a yellow border strip, 5 × 80½ inches, to one side edge of the quilt top.
2. Repeat on the opposite side. Press seams to one side.
3. Next, join the remaining 2 yellow border strips to the top and bottom edges of the quilt in the same way.
4. Press seams to one side.

To prepare backing

1. Cut the backing fabric in half lengthwise so you have two pieces, each 45 × 72 inches.
2. With right sides facing, join the two pieces along one long edge to make one piece 72 × 89½ inches.

To quilt

1. Beginning at the outer edge of the quilt top, use a quilt marker and ruler to rule off and mark ½-inch lines on all outside borders.

2. With wrong sides facing and batting between, pin the backing, batting, and quilt top together.

3. Beginning at the center and working outward in a sunburst pattern, take long, loose basting stitches through all three layers.

4. Using a small running stitch, quilt ¼ inch from each side of all seam lines and along all marked border lines, stopping short of the seam allowance around the outside edge of the quilt.

To finish

1. When all quilting is complete, remove all basting stitches.

2. Trim the batting ¼ inch smaller than the quilt top all around.

3. Trim the backing to same size as the quilt top.

4. Turn the raw edges of the quilt top to the inside ¼ inch and press. Turn the raw edges of the backing to the inside ¼ inch and press.

5. Slipstitch or machine stitch all around to finish.

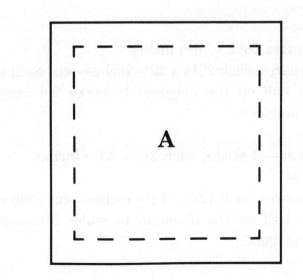

Delectable Mountains

While having a decidedly Southwestern feeling, this pattern is right at home in this 1800s New England Quaker-style house. The use of the same small-print fabric in two different colors makes this wallhanging quite dramatic. The finished size is 47 × 47 inches.

Materials
(all fabric is 45 inches wide)
1 yard tan fabric
3 yards blue fabric
quilt batting 48 × 48 inches
tracing paper
cardboard
quilt marker

Directions
Note: All measurements include a ¼-inch seam allowance.

Trace patterns A, B, and C and transfer to cardboard to make templates (see page 19). Cut out.

Cut the following
from blue

       A—24

       B—4

       C—4

       1 square 16½ × 16½ inches

       2 squares, each 22⅛ × 22⅛ inches—cut each square in half on the diagonal to make 2 triangles (4 triangles)

from tan

       borders—4 strips, each 2½ × 43½ inches

       A—24

       2 squares, each 12⅛ × 12⅛ inches—cut each square in half on the diagonal to make 2 triangles (4 triangles)

To make triangle borders

Refer to Figure 1a.

1. With right sides facing, join a tan triangle A to a blue triangle A along the long edge as shown.

2. Press seam to one side.

3. To make unit 1, refer to Figure 1b. Arrange 3 of these sets as shown and with right sides facing and edges aligned, join to make a row. Press seams to one side. Make 4 units this way.

4. Refer to Figure 1c and join 3 sets of blue/tan squares to make unit 2. Press seams to one side. Make 4 units this way.

5. Refer to Figure 2. With right sides facing, join unit 1 to unit 2 along the side edge. Press seam to one side. Make 4 in this way.

6. Refer to Figure 3. With right sides facing, join a blue B square to the left-side edge of one strip of squares as shown. Press seam to one side.

7. Next, with right sides facing, join a blue B square to the right-side edge of this strip. Press seam to one side. Make 2 in this way.

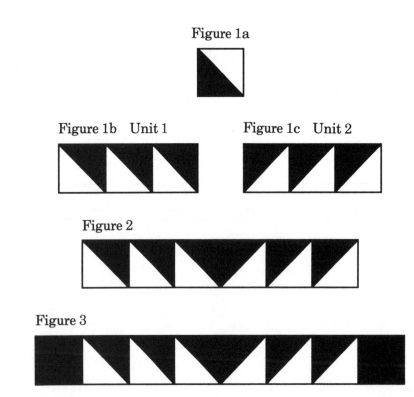

Figure 1a

Figure 1b   Unit 1

Figure 1c   Unit 2

Figure 2

Figure 3

To assemble block

Refer to Figure 4.

1. With right sides facing, join a tan triangle (made from the squares) to each side edge of the 16½-×-16½-inch tan square. Press seams to one side.

2. Refer to Figure 5. With right sides facing, join a unit made in Figure 2 to one raw edge of this pieced square. Press seam to one side.

3. Repeat on the opposite side as shown.

4. Refer to Figure 6. With right sides facing, join each unit made in Figure 3 to the remaining side edges of the pieced square to complete the triangle border.

5. Refer to Figure 7. With right sides facing, join a large blue triangle to each raw edge of the pieced square made in Figure 6. Press seams to one side.

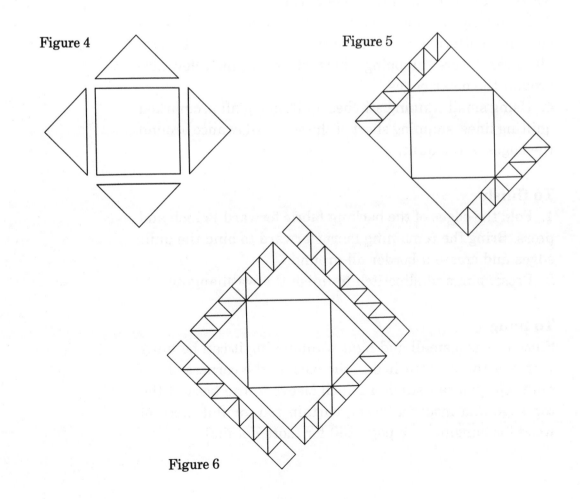

Figure 4

Figure 5

Figure 6

To make outer borders

Refer to Figure 8.

1. With right sides facing, join a blue C square to the left-side edge of a tan border strip 2½ × 43 inches. Press seam to one side.

2. Repeat on the opposite end of the strip. Make 2 in this way.

3. With right sides facing, join one of the remaining tan border strips to one side edge of the pieced square. Press seam to one side.

4. Repeat on the opposite side edge.

5. With right sides facing, join the long border strips to the top and bottom edges to complete the quilt top.

To quilt

1. Measure and mark a 2-inch grid over each color area.

2. With wrong sides facing and batting between, pin backing, batting, and quilt top together. There will be extra backing fabric all around. Do not trim.

3. Beginning at the center and working outward in a sunburst pattern, take long, loose, basting stitches through all three layers, stopping short of the seam allowance around the outer edges.

4. Using small running stitches, quilt along all premarked quilting lines, stopping short of the seam allowance around the edges of the quilt.

To finish

1. Fold the edges of the backing fabric forward ¼ inch and press. Bring the remaining fabric forward to bind the quilt edges and create a border all around.

2. Press, pin, and slipstitch to finish the wallhanging.

To hang

Since this is a small and light wallhanging it can be hung with Velcro tabs attached to the back of the corners of the quilt. Or, you can stitch a 2-inch sleeve to the back of the top edge and insert a dowel, curtain rod, or flat piece of wood for hanging (see page 160 for more details).

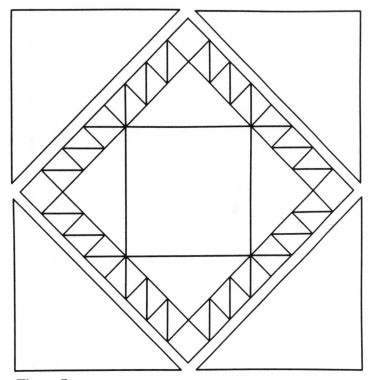

Figure 7

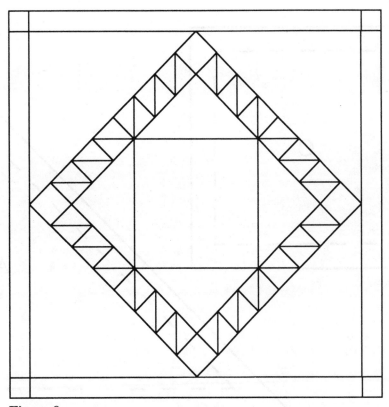

Figure 8

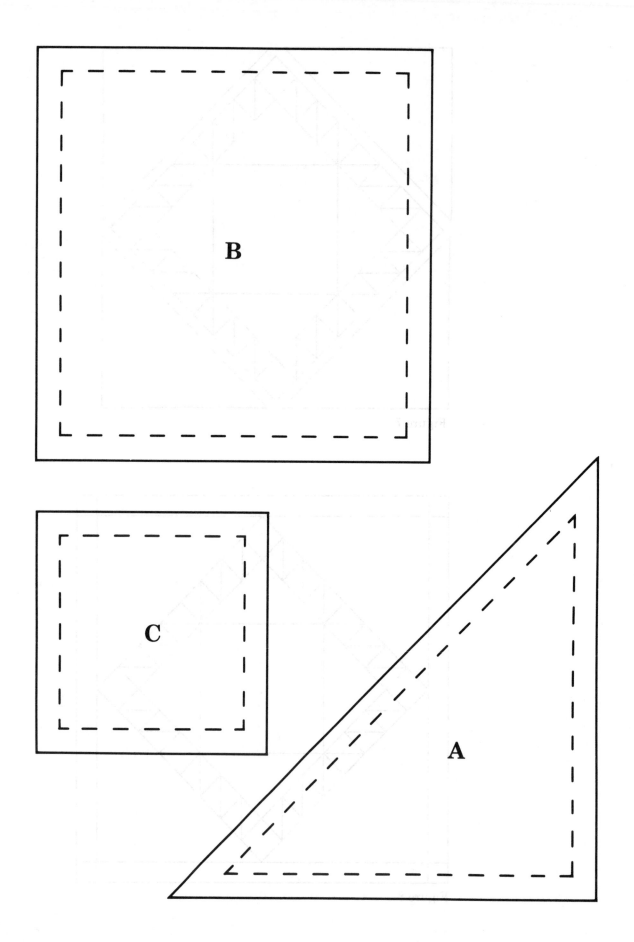

B

C

A

Flannel Checkerboard

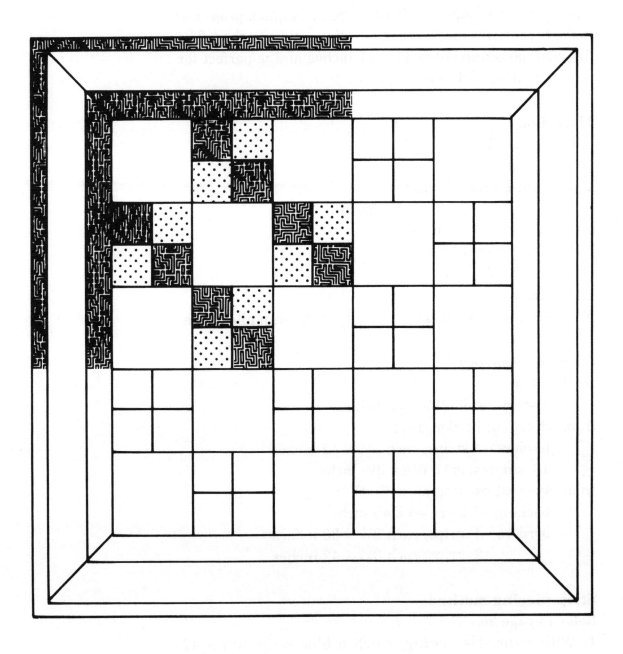

My daughter, Robby Savonen, has made many quilts for our books and as design director of our studio works with many creative quilters. She made this quilt with pieced baby-soft flannel squares. It's an especially quick project to make because it's made with the strip piecing method. The finished measurement is 41 × 41 inches and is perfect for wrapping around a new baby.

Materials
(all fabric is 45 inches wide)
¼ yard yellow flannel
1 yard white printed flannel
2 yards blue flannel (includes backing)
quilt batting 43 × 43 inches
1 skein white embroidery floss

Directions
Note: All measurements include a ¼-inch seam allowance.

Cut the following
from yellow
> 2 strips, each 3½ × 42 inches

from white (cut borders first)
> borders—4 strips, each 3½ × 42 inches
> 13 squares, each 6½ × 6½ inches

from blue (cut backing piece first)
> backing—1 piece 45 × 45 inches
> borders—4 strips, each 2½ × 36 inches
> 2 strips, each 3½ × 42 inches

Strip piecing method
Refer to page 25.

1. With right sides facing, stitch a blue strip, 3½ × 42 inches, to a yellow strip of the same size along one long edge.

2. Repeat with the other blue and yellow strips of the same size. Press seams to one side.

3. Measure and mark across the strips in 3½-inch segments. Cut on the marked lines to make 24 segments.

To make a block

1. Refer to Figure 1a and arrange two of the blue/yellow segments as shown.
2. Refer to Figure 1b. With right sides facing, stitch the two segments together along one side edge as shown.
3. Press seams to one side. Make 12 blocks in this way.

Figure 1a

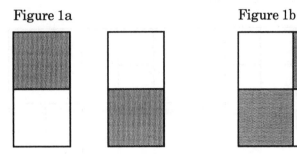

Figure 1b

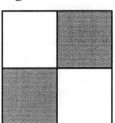

To make rows

Refer to Figure 2.

1. With right sides facing, stitch a white 6½-inch square to a block along the right-side edge. Press seam to one side.
2. Next, add another white square, then another block, followed by a white square, to make a row. Press seams to one side.
3. Make three rows in this way for rows 1, 3, and 5.
4. With right sides facing, stitch a block to a white square along the right-side edge. Press seam to one side.
5. Continue to join another block, then a white square, followed by another block. Press seams to one side.
6. Make two rows in this way for rows 2 and 4.

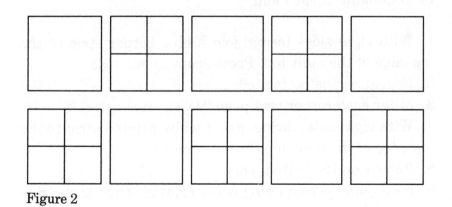

Figure 2

To join rows

Refer to Figure 3.

1. With right sides facing and seams aligned, join row 1 to row 2 along one long edge.

2. Continue to join all 5 rows in this way to make the quilt top.

3. Press seams to one side.

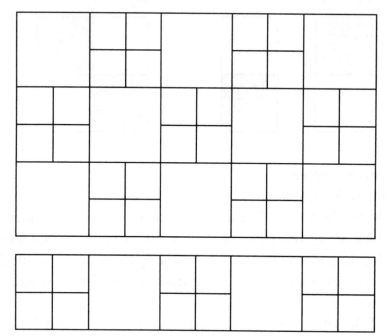

Figure 3

To add borders

Note: The border strips are all longer than needed to allow for the mitering of the corners. When adding borders, center each strip across the edge to be stitched, leaving an even amount at each end.

1. With right sides facing, join a blue border strip to the top edge of the quilt top. Press seam to one side.

2. Repeat on the bottom edge.

3. Miter each corner (see page 21).

4. With right sides facing, join a white printed strip to the top edge of the quilt top. Press seam to one side.

5. Repeat on the bottom edge.

6. Next, join the remaining white printed strips to the side edges of the quilt top.

7. Miter each corner.

To prepare quilt for tying

1. With wrong sides facing and batting between, pin the backing, batting, and quilt top together. There will be extra backing fabric all around.

2. Beginning at the center and working outward in a sunburst pattern, take long, loose, basting stitches through all three layers, stopping short of the seam allowance all around the outside edges.

To quilt

Note: This quilt is tied, but if you'd like to quilt the top you can do so by taking small running stitches on each side of all seam lines (see page 24).

1. Using the white embroidery floss, take a stitch down and then back up through all three layers at each corner of each block and printed square and every 6 inches along the outer seam of the blue border. Tie with a knot and cut, leaving ½-inch ends.

To finish

1. When all tying is complete, remove the basting stitches.

2. Trim the batting ¼ inch smaller than the quilt top all around.

3. Trim the backing to 1 inch larger than the quilt top all around.

4. Fold the raw edges of the backing forward ¼ inch and press.

5. Next, fold the backing forward onto the quilt top to create a ¼-inch border of blue all around. Press.

6. Slipstitch to the quilt top all around.

Flying Kites

Nancy Moore designed this 34-×-47-inch wallhanging that can also be used as a crib quilt. The blocks are made up of blue and white triangles, and the quilt is tied at random with blue embroidery floss.

Materials
(all fabric is 45 inches wide except the muslin, which is 60 inches wide)
¼ yard each of 4 different blue prints
2 yards bleached muslin
quilt batting 36 × 48 inches
1 skein blue embroidery floss
tracing paper
cardboard

Directions
Note: All measurements include a ¼-inch seam allowance. Trace pattern A and transfer to cardboard to make a template (see page 19). Cut out.

Cut the following
from each blue print
  A—12 (total of 48 A pieces)
from muslin (cut backing piece first)
  backing—1 piece 36 × 50 inches
  2 strips, each 2½ × 47½ inches
  5 lattice strips, each 3½ × 30½ inches
  8 lattice strips, each 3½ × 8½ inches
  A—48

To make squares
Refer to Figure 1.

1. With right sides facing, join a blue A print piece to a muslin A piece along the diagonal to make a square.

2. Press seam to one side. Make 48 squares in this way.

Figure 1

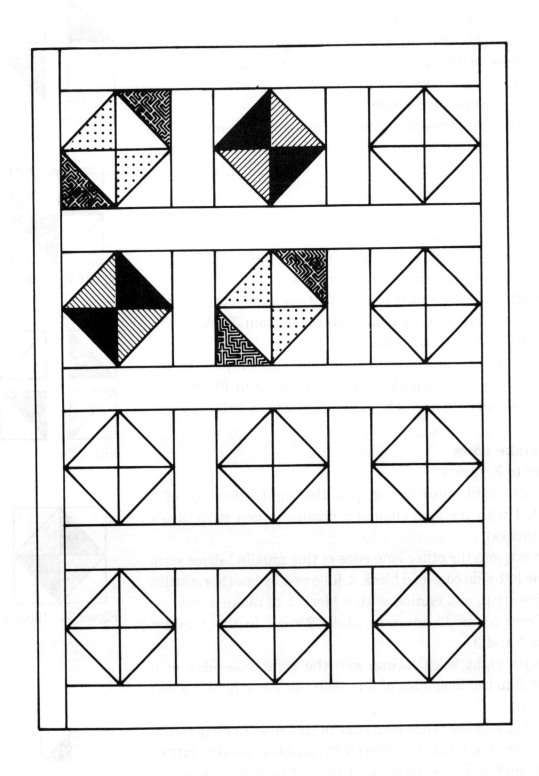

To make block 1
Refer to Figures 2a and 2b.

1. Using 4 of the pieced squares (made from the same blue print) as shown in Figure 1, arrange as shown in Figure 2a.
2. With right sides facing and raw edges aligned, join the 2 squares in the top row together along one side edge. Repeat with the bottom 2 squares.
3. Press seams to one side.
4. With right sides facing and seams aligned, join the top and bottom rows to make block 1 as shown in Figure 2b.
5. Press seam to one side. Make 6 blocks in this way.

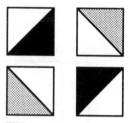

Figure 2a

To make block 2
Refer to Figures 3a and 3b.

1. Using 4 of the pieced squares (made from the same blue print), arrange as shown in Figure 3a.
2. With right sides facing, join the 2 squares in the top row along one side edge. Repeat with the bottom 2 squares.
3. Press seams to one side.
4. With right sides facing and seams aligned, join the top and bottom rows to make block 2 as shown in Figure 3b.
5. Press seam to one side. Make 6 blocks in this way.

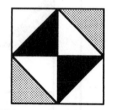

Figure 2b   Block 1

To make rows
Refer to Figure 4.

1. With right sides facing, join the right-side edge of a block 1 with the long edge of a muslin lattice strip (3½ × 8½ inches).
2. Next, join the other long edge of this muslin lattice strip to the left-side edge of a block 2, followed by another muslin lattice strip, and ending with a block 1 to make a row
3. Press seams to one side. Make 2 rows in this way for rows 1 and 3.
4. With right sides facing, join the right-side edge of a block 2 to the long edge of a muslin lattice strip (3½ × 8½ inches).
5. Next, join the other long edge of this muslin strip to the left side of a block 1, followed by another muslin lattice strip, and ending with another block 2 to make a row.
6. Press seams to one side. Make 2 rows in this way for rows 2 and 4.

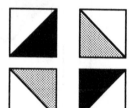

Figure 3a

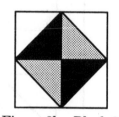

Figure 3b   Block 2

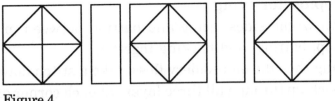

Figure 4

To join rows

Refer to Figure 5.

1. With right sides facing, join a muslin lattice strip 3½ × 30½ inches to the top edge of row 1.

2. Next, join another muslin lattice strip to the bottom edge of row 1.

3. Continue to join all 4 rows, each separated by a muslin lattice strip in this way, and ending with a muslin lattice strip at the bottom of row 4.

4. Press seams to one side.

5. With right sides facing, join the remaining 2 muslin lattice strips to each side of the quilt top.

6. Press seams to one side.

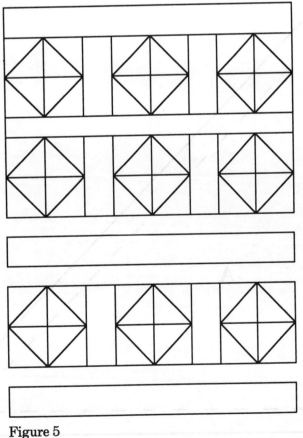

Figure 5

To prepare for tying

1. With wrong sides facing and batting between, pin the quilt top, batting, and backing together.

2. Using the blue embroidery floss, take a stitch down and then back up through all three layers at each corner of each square in each block. Tie with a knot and cut, leaving ½-inch ends. Continue to tie the quilt at various intervals along the lattice strips.

To finish

1. When all tying is complete, remove the pins.

2. Trim the batting to ¼ inch smaller than the quilt top all around.

3. Fold the raw edges of the backing forward ¼ inch and press. Turn the edges forward ¼ inch onto the front of the quilt top and press. Pin all around.

4. Slipstitch to the quilt top to finish.

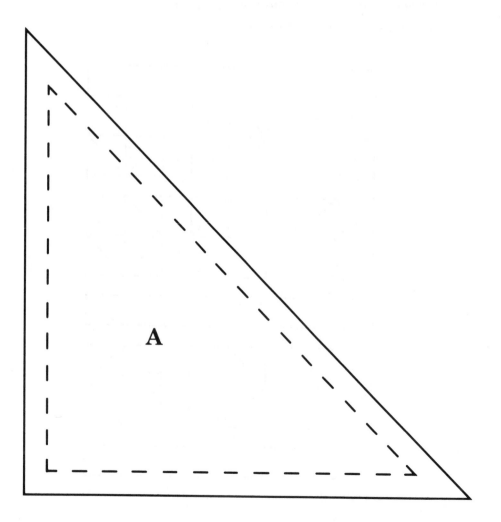

Friendship Ring

Sometimes referred to as Hopscotch, this pattern is quite interesting, and although it may look difficult to make, it employs strip piecing as well as the quick-and-easy triangle method, which makes the piecing quite easy. While it looks as if there are lots of small blocks stitched together to make the quilt top, there are only three rows, each made up of two large blocks.

The soft pink and green colors are appealing for use in a bedroom, and, Robby Savonen, made this single-bed-size quilt by combining solids and calico prints. The finished quilt measures 50 × 68 inches. To enlarge it, simply add more blocks and rows or another border all around.

Materials
(all fabric is 45 inches wide)
1 yard rose print fabric
2 yards pink solid fabric
2 yards white fabric
2 yards green print fabric
3 yards backing fabric (or 2 yards 60-inch-wide muslin)
quilt batting 54 × 72 inches
tracing paper
cardboard
quilt marker

Directions
Note: All measurements include a ¼-inch seam allowance.

Trace patterns A and B and transfer to cardboard to make templates (see page 19). Cut out.

Cut the following
from rose print
      1 piece 18 × 26 inches
      1 strip 2½ × 30 inches
      1 strip 2½ × 15 inches

from pink (cut the borders first)
      borders—2 strips, each 2½ × 58½ inches
            2 strips, each 2½ × 36½ inches
            8 strips, each 2½ × 39 inches

from white (cut the borders first)

        borders—2 strips, each 2½ × 62½ inches

                  2 strips, each 2½ × 40½ inches

    1 piece 18 × 26 inches

    4 strips, each 2½ × 39 inches

    2 strips, each 2½ × 30 inches

    1 strip 2½ × 15 inches

    A—100

    B—4

from green print (cut borders first)

        borders—2 strips, each 3½ × 68½ inches

                  2 strips, each 3½ × 44½ inches

For units 1 and 2 use the strip piecing method (see page 25).

Unit 1

1. With right sides facing, stitch a solid pink strip 2½ × 39 inches along one long edge of a white strip of the same size.
2. Next, join a white strip to the pink strip.
3. Press seams to one side. Make 4 sets of 3 strips each in this way.
4. Measure and mark across each set of strips every 6½ inches. Cut on the marked lines to make 24 sets of unit 1 as shown in Figure 1.

Figure 1

Unit 2

1. With right sides facing, stitch a rose print strip 2½ × 15 inches along one long edge of a white strip of the same size.
2. Next, join another rose print strip to the white strip. Press seams to one side.
3. Measure and mark off 2½-inch segments. Cut on all marked lines to make a total of 6 segments.
4. With right sides facing, join a white strip 2½ × 30 inches

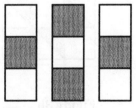

Figure 2a

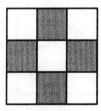

Figure 2b

to one long edge of a rose strip of the same size. Then join another white strip to the rose strip.

5. Press seams to one side.

6. Measure and mark off 2½-inch segments. Cut on the marked lines to make a total of 12 segments.

7. Refer to Figure 2a to arrange 3 sets of segments. With right sides facing, join the 3 segments to make unit 2 as shown in Figure 2b.

8. Press seams to one side. Make 6 of unit 2.

Unit 3

For unit 3 use the quick-and-easy triangle method (see page 26).

1. On the wrong side of the white piece 18 × 26 inches, measure and mark a grid of 40 squares, each 2⅞ × 2⅞ inches, so you have 8 across and 5 down.

2. Draw a diagonal line through all the squares.

3. With right sides facing, pin the marked white piece to the rose print fabric of the same size. Stitch ¼ inch from each side of all diagonal lines. Cut on the solid lines to make 80 squares of white-and-rose triangles.

4. Press seams to one side.

5. Refer to Figure 3a and arrange 5 of the white A pieces with 4 of the pieced squares to form 3 rows of 3 squares each.

6. With right sides facing and edges aligned, join the 3 squares in each row. Press seams to one side.

7. Refer to Figure 3b. With right sides facing and seams aligned, join row 1 and row 2 along one long edge, followed by row 3 to make unit 3 as shown.

8. Press seams to one side. Make 20 of unit 3.

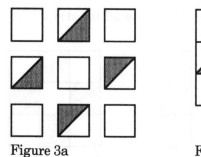

Figure 3a

Figure 3b

To make block 1

Refer to Figures 4a and 4b.

1. Using one white B square, 4 of unit 1, 1 of unit 2, and 3 of unit 3, arrange into 3 rows of 3 units each as shown in Figure 4a.

2. With right sides facing, join the 3 units in each row.

3. Press seams to one side.

4. With right sides facing and seams aligned, join the 3 rows to make block 1 as shown in Figure 4b.

5. Press seams to one side. Make 4 of block 1.

To make block 2

Refer to Figure 4c.

1. Follow directions for block 1, substituting a unit 3 in the top left corner for the white B square, as shown in Figure 4c.

2. Make 2 of block 2.

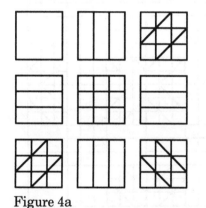

Figure 4a

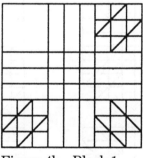

Figure 4b   Block 1

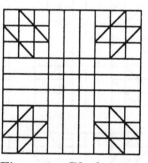

Figure 4c   Block 2

To make rows

Refer to Figure 5 for placement of blocks.

1. With right sides facing and seams aligned, stitch 2 of block 1 together along one side edge to make the top row.

2. Press seam to one side.

3. With right sides facing and seams aligned, stitch 2 of block 2 together along one side edge to make the middle row.

4. Press seam to one side.

5. With right sides facing and seams aligned, stitch a block 1 to another block 1 along one side to make the bottom row.

6. Press seam to one side.

To join rows

Refer to Figure 6.

1. With right sides facing and seams aligned, join the bottom edge of the top row with the top edge of the middle row.

2. Next, join the bottom edge of the middle row to the top edge of the bottom row to make the quilt top.

3. Press seams to one side.

Figure 5

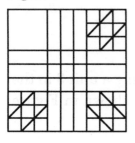 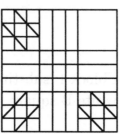

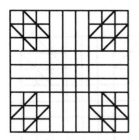 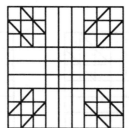

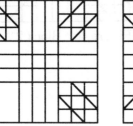 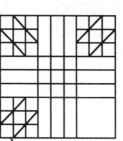

Figure 6

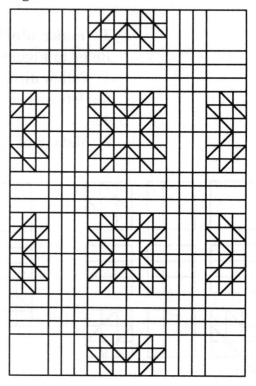

To join borders

1. With right sides facing, join a 2½-×-36½-inch pink border strip to the top raw edge of the quilt top. Repeat on the bottom edge of the quilt.

2. Press seams to one side.

3. Next, join the remaining pink border strips to each side edge of the quilt top in the same way. Press seams to one side.

4. With right sides facing, join the shorter white border strips to the top and bottom edges of the quilt top in the same way. Press seams to one side.

5. Stitch the remaining white border strips to each side edge of the quilt top. Press seams to one side.

6. With right sides facing, join a 3½ × 44½ inch border strip to the top edge of the quilt top in the same way. Repeat on the bottom edge. Press seams to one side.

7. Stitch the remaining green border strips to each side edge of the quilt top. Press seams to one side.

To prepare the backing

Note: If using 60-inch-wide muslin for backing, no preparation is necessary.

1. Cut the backing fabric in half lengthwise to make 2 pieces, each 45 × 54 inches.

2. With right sides facing, join the 2 pieces along one long edge to make a piece 54 × 90 inches. Press seam to one side. To avoid a center seam see page 18 for piecing directions.

To prepare for quilting

1. Trace the heart quilting pattern and transfer it to each large white corner square (see page 19).

2. Transfer the connecting heart pattern to the borders.

3. Mark connecting diagonal lines through all the small white squares in each block.

4. With wrong sides facing, pin the backing fabric, batting, and quilt top together.

5. Beginning at the center of the top and working outward in a sunburst pattern, take long, loose, basting stitches through all three layers, stopping short of the seam allowance around the edge of the quilt.

To quilt

1. Using small running stitches, quilt on all premarked lines and ¼ inch from each side of all seam lines. Do not quilt into seam allowances around the edges of the quilt top.

2. When all quilting is complete, remove the basting stitches.

To finish

1. Trim the batting ½ inch smaller than the quilt top all around.

2. Trim backing to the same size as the quilt top.

3. Turn the raw edges of the quilt top to the inside ¼ inch all around and press.

4. Turn the raw edges of the backing to the inside ¼ inch all around and press.

5. Slipstitch or machine stitch all around to finish.

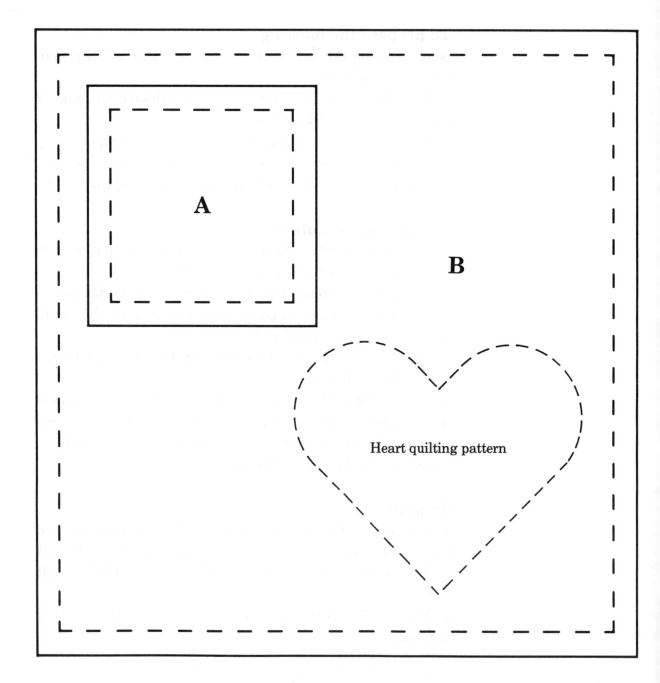

A

B

Heart quilting pattern

Amish Square

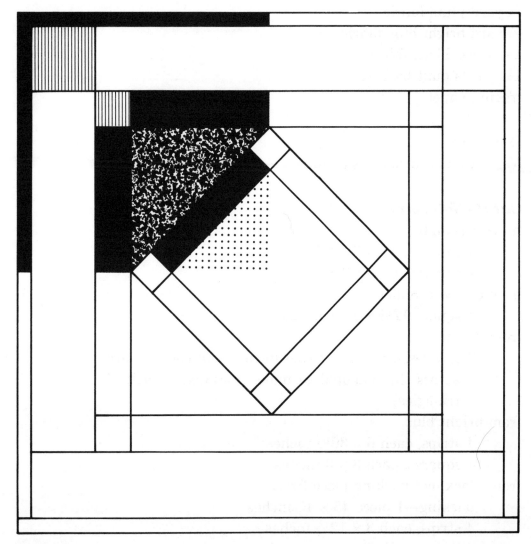

Figure 3

Amish quilts are always among the most popular designs. The colors often include red, lavender, green, blue, and black, and the designs are simple and straightforward. These quilts have a bold, graphic quality that is both traditional and contemporary in feeling. Use this quilt as a lap throw, a table cover, or a wallhanging. The finished size is 42 × 42 inches.

Materials
(all fabric is 45 inches wide)
¼ yard burgundy fabric
½ yard dusty lavender fabric
½ yard plum fabric
¾ yard bright blue fabric
1¾ yards black fabric
1½ yards quilt batting
tracing paper

Directions
Note: All measurements include a ¼-inch seam allowance.

Cut the following
from burgundy
>   4 squares, each 3½ × 3½ inches
>   4 squares, each 6 × 6 inches

from dusty lavender
>   1 square 12½ × 12½ inches

from plum
>   2 squares, each 12⅞ × 12⅞ inches—cut each square
>   across the diagonal to make 2 triangles each (4
>   triangles)

from bright blue
>   4 strips, each 6 × 30½ inches
>   4 squares, each 3 × 3 inches

from black (cut backing piece first)
>   backing—1 piece 45 × 45 inches
>   4 strips, each 3 × 12½ inches
>   4 strips, each 3½ × 24½ inches

To make the quilt top
1. With right sides facing, join a short black strip (3 × 12½ inches) to each side of the dusty lavender square. Press seams to one side.
2. With right sides facing, join a bright blue square to each short end of the remaining 2 shorter black strips to make 2 longer strips.
3. Next, stitch one of these long strips to the top edge of the

dusty lavender square and another strip to the bottom edge to make a larger square as shown in Figure 1.

4. Press seams to one side.

5. With right sides facing, stitch the diagonal edge of a plum triangle to each of the 4 edges of this larger square.

6. Press seams to one side.

7. With right sides facing, join a black strip (3½ × 24½ inches) to each side of this square. Press seams to one side.

8. Next, stitch a small burgundy square to each short end of the remaining 2 black strips to make 2 longer strips.

9. With right sides facing, stitch one of these longer strips to the top edge and another to the bottom edge of the square as shown in Figure 2.

10. Press seams to one side.

11. With right sides facing, stitch a bright blue strip to each side of the square. Press seams to one side.

12. Next, join a large burgundy square to each short end of the remaining 2 bright blue strips to make 2 longer strips.

13. With right sides facing, stitch one of these longer strips to the top edge and another to the bottom edge to complete the quilt top as shown in Figure 3.

14. Press seams to one side.

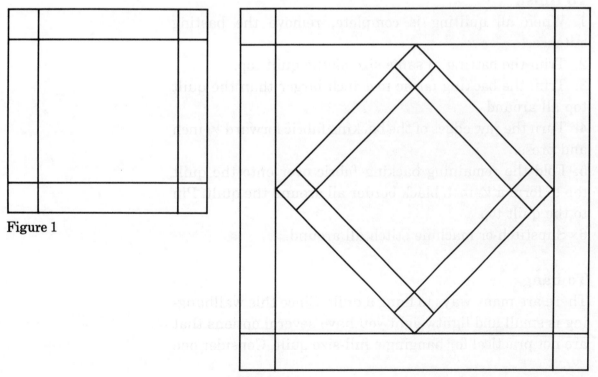

Figure 1

Figure 2

Preparing to quilt

Refer to page 19 to transfer quilt patterns.

1. Trace the quilt patterns 1–7. Transfer pattern 1 to the center of the dusty lavender square.

2. Next, transfer pattern 2 to the shorter black border strips.

3. Transfer pattern 3 to the blue squares.

4. Transfer pattern 4 to the plum triangles.

5. Transfer pattern 5 to the larger black borders and continue this pattern through the small burgundy squares.

6. Transfer pattern 6 to the large burgundy squares and pattern 7 to the blue borders.

To quilt

1. With wrong sides facing and batting between, pin backing, batting, and quilt top together.

2. Beginning at the center and working outward in a sunburst pattern, take long, loose basting stitches through all three layers.

3. Using small running stitches, quilt along all the pre-marked quilting lines.

To finish

1. When all quilting is complete, remove the basting stitches.

2. Trim the batting to same size as the quilt top.

3. Trim the backing fabric to 1 inch larger than the quilt top all around.

4. Turn the raw edges of the backing fabric forward ¼ inch and press.

5. Fold the remaining backing fabric over onto the quilt top to form a ½-inch black border all around the quilt. Pin to the quilt top.

6. Slipstitch or machine stitch all around.

To hang

There are many ways to hang a quilt. Since this wallhanging is small and lightweight you have several options that are not practical for hanging a full-size quilt. Consider one of the following that will work best for the area where the wallhanging will be placed:

1. You can attach a small Velcro tab to the back of each corner of the quilt and another in the center of each side edge. Then attach the corresponding tabs to the wall and position the wallhanging firmly to the wall.

2. Another method is to sew a muslin sleeve to the backing across the top of the quilt. Insert a dowel, curtain rod, or flat piece of wood through the sleeve. The insert should be slightly longer than the quilt so that it can be suspended on brackets.

3. The third method is to attach Velcro strips to a wooden frame such as artist's stretcher bars the same size as the wallhanging. Then attach corresponding Velcro strips to the back of the quilt and hang the frame where desired.

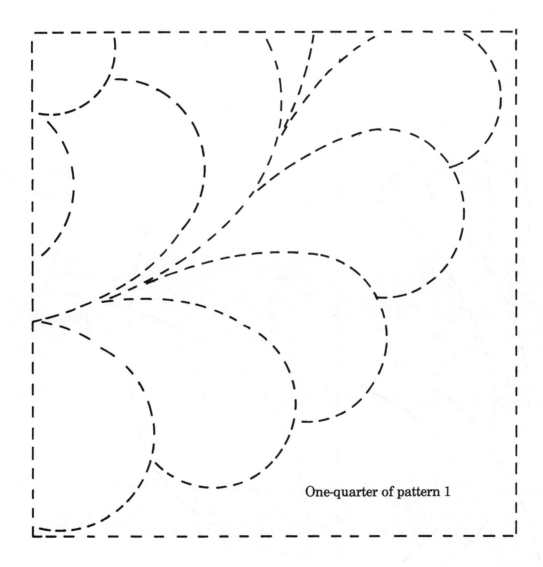

One-quarter of pattern 1

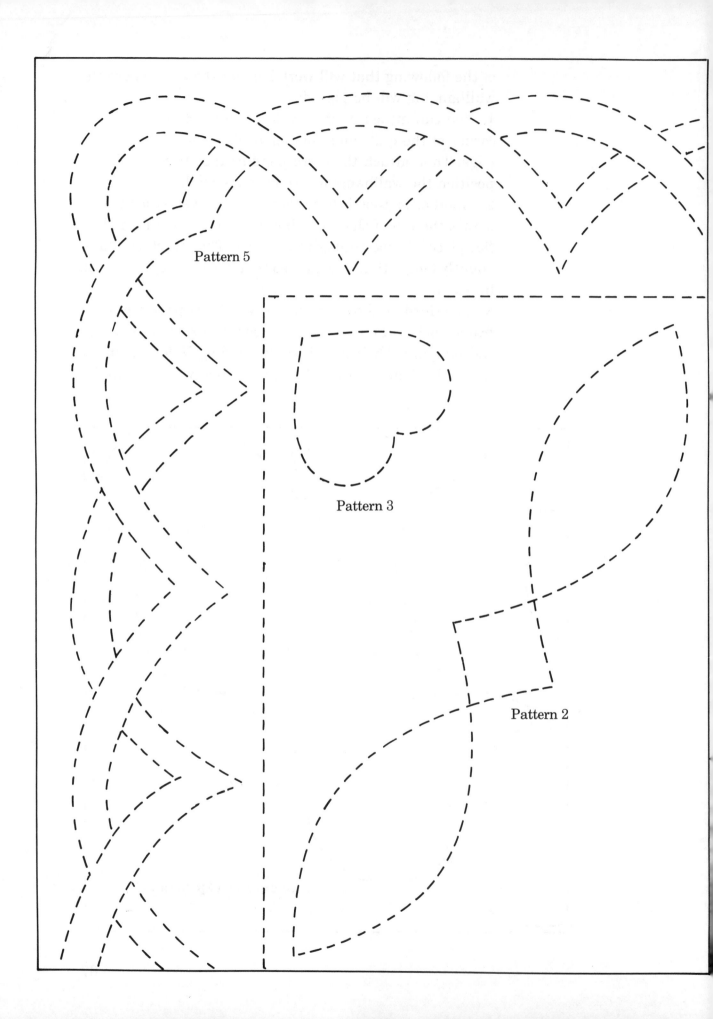

Pattern 5

Pattern 3

Pattern 2

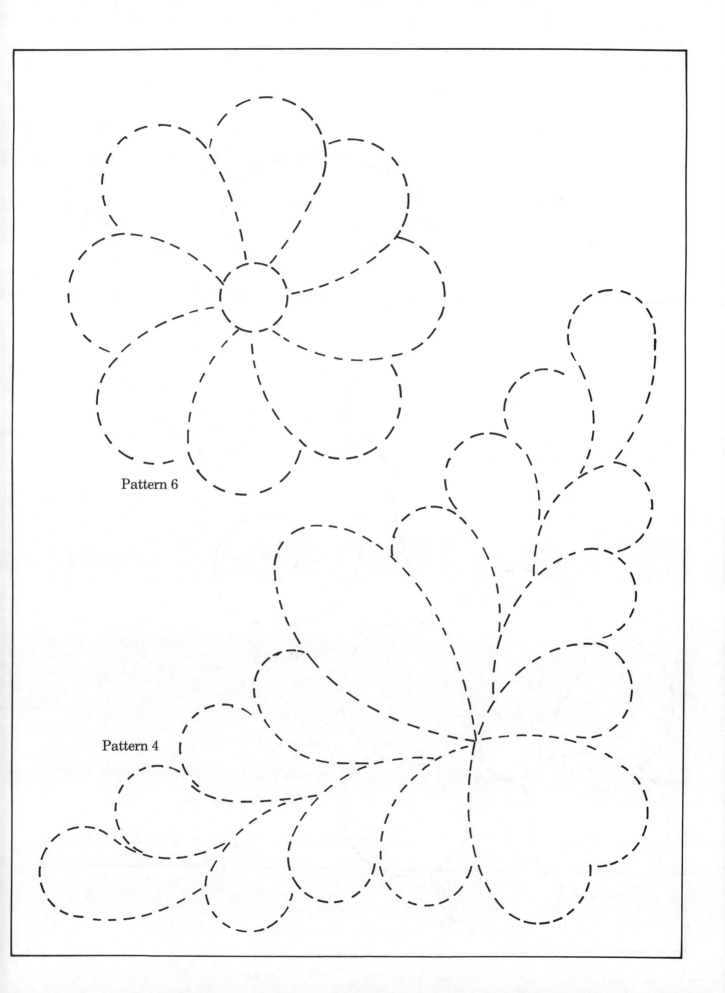

Pattern 6

Pattern 4

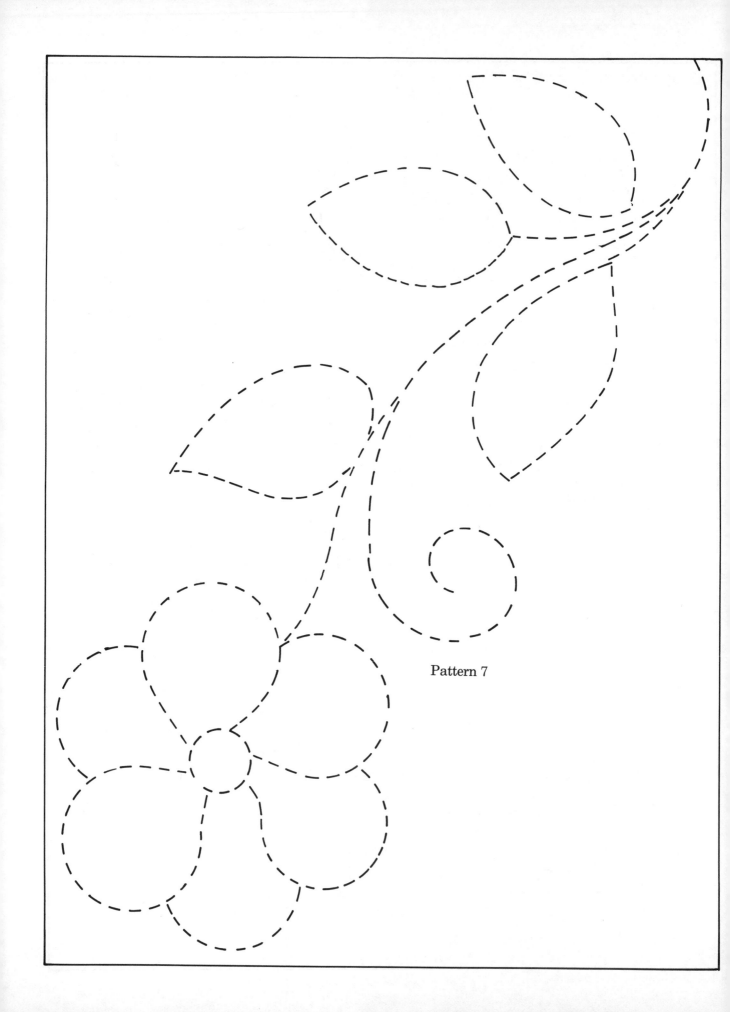

Pattern 7

Sunshine Star Tablecover

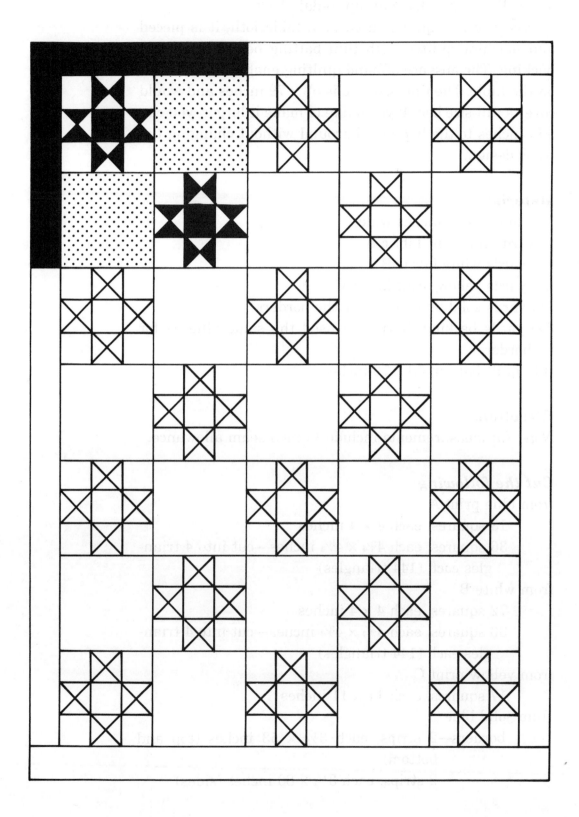

This patchwork tablecover was made with Waverly fabric called "Provence." While it is traditional in feeling, the blue and yellow prints have an up-to-date look.

Because this quilt is used as a tablecloth, it is pieced and machine quilted with thin batting between top and backing. The absence of hand quilting enables it to lie flat on the table. The finished size is 58 × 79 inches and would cover a full-size bed. If you'd like to make it larger, you can add inches to the border all around without changing the basic design.

Materials
(all fabric is 45 inches wide)
¾ yard blue print fabric A
1½ yards white fabric B
1¾ yards yellow print fabric C
2¼ yards solid blue fabric for the borders
3½ yards backing fabric (we used the same blue as for borders)
thin quilt batting 58 × 79 inches

Directions
Note: All measurements include ¼-inch seam allowance.

Cut the following
from blue print A

      18 squares, each 4 × 4 inches

      36 squares, each 4¾ × 4¾ inches—cut into 4 triangles each (144 triangles)

from white B

      72 squares, each 4 × 4 inches

      36 squares, each 4¾ × 4¾ inches—cut into 4 triangles each (144 triangles)

from yellow print C

      17 squares, each 11 × 11 inches

from solid blue

      borders—2 strips, each 3¼ × 53 inches (top and bottom)

            2 strips, each 3¼ × 80 inches (sides)

To make a block

1. With right sides facing, join an A triangle to a B triangle along one short side to make a larger triangle. Press seam to one side. Make 8 in this way.

2. Refer to Figure 1 and join 2 larger triangles together to make a square as shown. Press seam to one side. Make 4 squares in this way.

3. With right sides facing, join a B square to a white-and-blue triangle square and then another B square to make a row. Press seams to one side.

4. Next, join a white-and-blue triangle square to a B square and then add another white-and-blue triangle square to make row 2. Press seams to one side.

5. Repeat step 3 to make the third row.

6. Refer to Figure 2. With right sides facing and seams aligned, stitch the three rows together to make a block as shown. Make 18 blocks in this way. Press seams to one side.

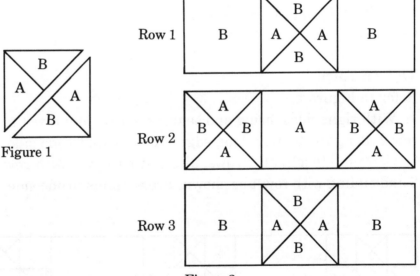

Figure 1

Row 1

Row 2

Row 3

Figure 2

To make row 1

Refer to Figure 3.

1. With right sides facing and seams aligned, stitch a quilt block to a C square along the right-side edge. Press seam to one side.

2. Next, join a block, then a C square, and end the row with another block. Press seams to one side. Make 4 in this way.

Figure 3

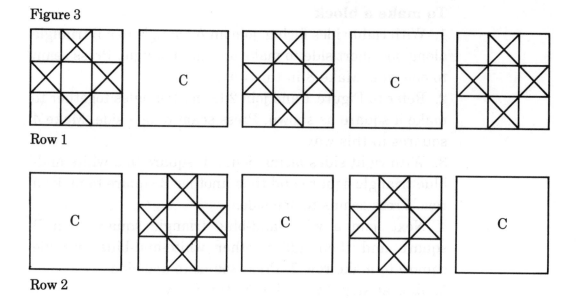

Row 1

Row 2

To make row 2

1. With right sides facing, join a C square to a quilt block along the right-side edge. Press seam to one side.
2. Next, join another C square, then a block, and end the row with a C square. Press seams to one side. Make 3 in this way.

To join rows

Refer to Figure 4.

1. With right sides facing and seams aligned, join row 1 to row 2 along the bottom, long edge. Press seam to one side.
2. Continue to join all 7 rows, alternating row 1 with row 2 and ending with row 1 as shown. Press seams to one side.

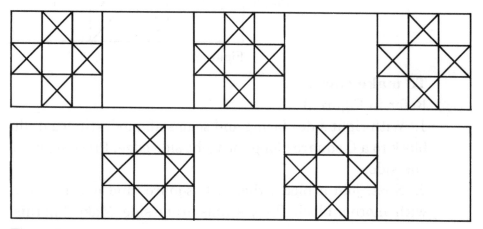

Figure 4

To join borders

1. With right sides facing and seams aligned, join the top border strip to the top edge of the patchwork. Press seams to one side.

2. Repeat with bottom border strip.

3. Next, join side border strips to each side edge in the same way.

To finish

1. Cut the batting ½ inch smaller than the patchwork top all around.

2. Cut the backing fabric in half so you have 2 pieces, each 1¾ yards.

3. With right sides facing and raw edges aligned, stitch the 2 backing pieces together along one long edge. Open seam and press. If you'd rather have the seams at either side, rather than in the center of the back, cut one of the backing pieces in half lengthwise to create 2 narrow strips and attach them to each side edge of the 45-inch wide panel. Open seams and press.

4. Trim the backing to the same size as the top.

5. With wrong sides facing and batting between, pin backing, batting, and top together.

6. Beginning at the center and moving outward in a sunburst pattern, take long, loose basting stitches through all three layers, stopping short of the seam allowance around the outside edges.

7. Turn the raw edges of the backing under ¼ inch and press. Turn the raw edges of the top to the inside ¼ inch and press.

8. Machine stitch all around and remove basting stitches to finish the tablecover.

To quilt

1. If you'd like to hand quilt this project, begin at the center of the patchwork and work outward, taking small running stitches ¼ inch from each side of all seam lines.

2. To machine quilt, stitch along each seam line with same thread used to piece the top.

Pink Sails

This is a familiar pattern, usually made with shades of blue and used in a boy's room. The use of pink and white is different and makes this a delightfully feminine quilt as well as a pretty wallhanging. The finished measurement is 76 × 88 inches. While this is a full-size quilt, the quick-and-easy triangle method is used as a shortcut to piecing triangles into squares.

Materials
(all fabric is 45 inches wide)
2 yards white fabric
4½ yards pink fabric
5 yards backing fabric
quilt batting 76 × 88 inches
quilt marker

Directions
Note: All measurements include a ¼-inch seam allowance.

Cut the following
from white A
> borders (cut border strips vertically first)
>> 4 strips, each 3½ × 60½ inches
> 1 piece 25 × 30 inches
> 13 rectangles, each 3½ × 12½ inches
> 26 rectangles 3½ × 6½ inches

from pink B
> borders (cut border strips vertically first)
>> 2 strips, each 3½ × 60½ inches
>> 2 strips, each 8½ × 76½ inches
>> 2 strips, each 3½ × 88½ inches
> 1 rectangle 25 × 30 inches
> 13 rectangles, each 3½ × 6½ inches
> 12 squares, each 12½ × 12½ inches

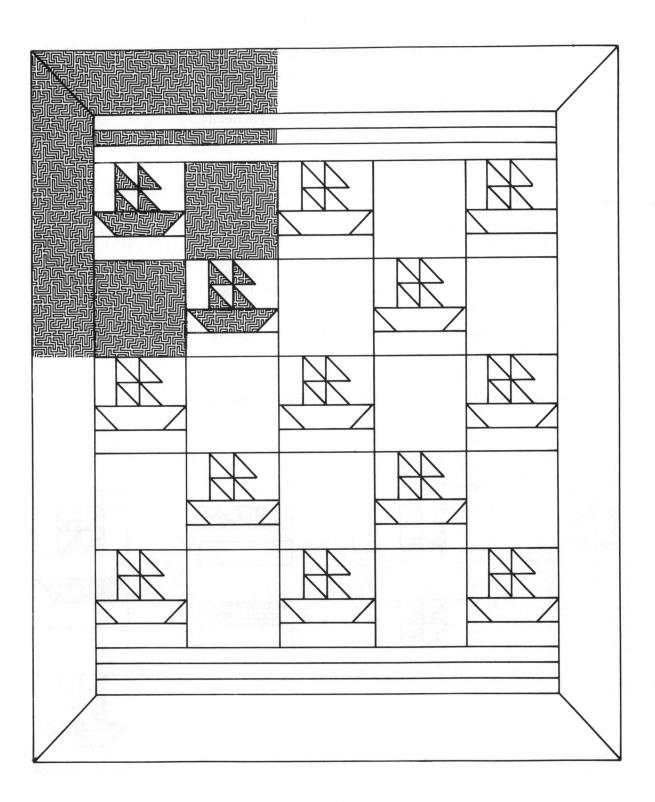

Quick-and-easy triangle method

1. On the wrong side of the white fabric, measure and mark a grid of squares, each 3⅞ × 3⅞ inches, to create 6 rows of 7 squares each.

2. With right sides facing, pin the marked fabric to the same size pink fabric and refer to page 26 for quick-and-easy stitching.

3. You will have 84 pink-and-white squares. You'll need only 78; however, it's always good to have a few extras.

To make sailboat block

Refer to Figure 1.

1. With right sides facing, join 4 pink-and-white squares as shown. Press seams to one side.

2. Refer to Figure 2. With right sides facing, join a 3½-×-6½-inch pink B rectangle to the left-side edge of the pieced squares. Press seam to one side.

3. Repeat on the opposite side edge in the same way to complete the top half of the sailboat block.

4. Refer to Figure 3. With right sides facing, join a pink-and-white square to a 3½-×-6½-inch pink B rectangle along

Figure 1

Figure 2

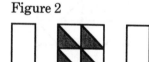

Figure 3

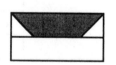

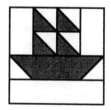

Figure 4

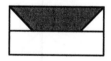

one short end, followed by another pink-and-white square as shown. Press seams to one side.

5. Next, join this strip to a white A 3½-×-12½-inch rectangle along a long edge as shown. Press seam to one side to complete the bottom half of the block.

6. Refer to Figure 4. With right sides facing and seams aligned, join the top and bottom halves of the block. Press seam to one side. Make 13 blocks in this way.

To make rows

Refer to Figure 5.

1. With right sides facing and raw edges aligned, join a sailboat block to a pink B square, 12½ × 12½ inches, along the right-side edge. Press seam to one side.

2. On the other side of the square, continue by joining a sailboat block followed by a pink B square and ending the row with another sailboat block. Press all seams to one side. Make 3 rows in this way for rows 1, 3, and 5.

3. To make row 2, begin with a pink B square, then a sailboat block, followed by a pink B square, another sailboat block, and ending with a pink B square. Press seams to one side. Make 2 rows in this way for rows 2 and 4.

Figure 5

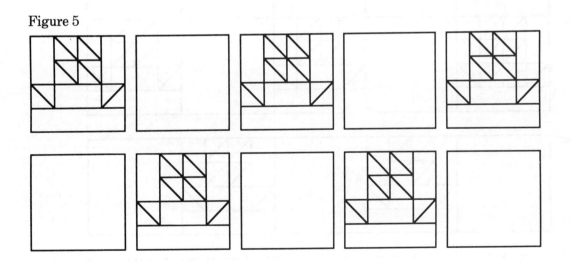

To join rows
Refer to Figure 6.

1. With right sides facing and seams aligned, join row 1 with row 2 along one long edge. Press seam to one side.

2. Continue to join rows in this way.

To join borders
Note: The borders on this quilt are mitered at the corners. See page 21 for doing this. However, square borders are easier to create, and the following directions are for square borders as seen on most of the other quilts in this book.

1. With right sides facing, join a white A strip, $3\frac{1}{2} \times 60\frac{1}{2}$ inches, to the bottom edge of the quilt top. Press seam to one side.

Figure 6

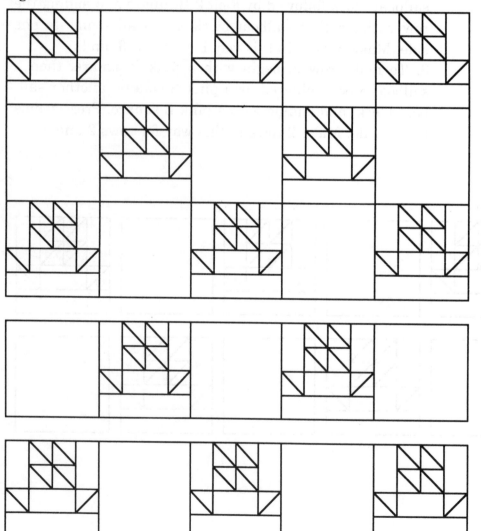

2. Repeat on the top edge of the quilt in the same way.

3. With right sides facing, join a pink B strip, $3\frac{1}{2} \times 60\frac{1}{2}$ inches, to the bottom edge of the quilt top. Press seams to one side.

4. Repeat on the top edge of the quilt in the same way.

5. Repeat steps 1 and 2.

6. With right sides facing, join a pink B strip, $8\frac{1}{2} \times 76\frac{1}{2}$ inches, to the bottom edge of the quilt top. Press seam to one side.

7. Repeat on the top edge of the quilt in the same way.

8. With right sides facing, join a pink B strip, $8\frac{1}{2} \times 88\frac{1}{2}$ to one side edge of the quilt top. Press seam to one side.

9. Repeat on the opposite side edge to complete the quilt top.

To quilt

Refer to page 19 for transferring quilt patterns.

1. Trace the quilt patterns and transfer to the quilt top. For a simpler quilt pattern, consider quilting along all seam lines and creating a diagonal grid of evenly spaced lines across the quilt borders.

2. With wrong sides facing and batting between, pin the backing, batting, and quilt top together. There will be extra backing fabric all around.

3. Beginning at the center and working outward in a sunburst pattern, take long, loose basting stitches through all three layers, stopping short of the seam allowance around the outer edges.

4. Using small running stitches, quilt along all premarked quilting lines or $\frac{1}{4}$ inch from each side of all seam lines. Do not quilt into the seam allowance around the quilt.

To finish

1. When all quilting is complete, remove basting stitches.

2. Trim the batting $\frac{1}{4}$ inch smaller than the quilt top all around.

3. Trim the backing to same size as quilt top.

4. Turn backing edges to inside $\frac{1}{4}$ inch and press.

5. Turn raw edges of quilt top to inside $\frac{1}{4}$ inch and press.

6. Slipstitch or machine stitch all around to finish.

Quilting Pattern for Boat

One-Half Quilting Pattern for Solid Square

Quilting Pattern for Border

Floral Frames

Large blocks of floral fabric are framed with bands of white and aqua-green lattice strips to make this pretty, soft bedroom quilt. The frames are joined with mitered corners for interest (see page 21 for making mitered corners). Mix any pretty floral pattern with solids that match. The color combination of soft green and peach are used here is always a restful color scheme for a bedroom. The built-in closets and wallpaper in the room echo the colors of the quilt, which is 77 × 95½ inches.

Materials
(all fabric is 45 inches wide)
2¾ yards green fabric
2¾ yards white fabric
3¼ yards floral fabric
5½ yards backing fabric
quilt batting 77 × 95½ inches

Directions
Note: All measurements include a ¼-inch seam allowance.

Cut the following
from floral
>   2 strips, each 3½ × 68½ inches (top and bottom borders)
>   2 strips, each 3½ × 90 inches (top and bottom borders)
>   31 squares, each 7½ × 7½ inches
>   9 squares, each 7⅞ × 7⅞ inches—cut each square in half on the diagonal to make 2 triangles (18 triangles)

from white
>   2 strips, each 2 × 62½ inches (top and bottom borders)
>   2 strips, each 2 × 81 inches (side borders)

Figure 5

2 strips, each 2 × 77 inches (top and bottom borders)

2 strips, each 2 × 96 inches (side borders)

80 strips, each 2 × 14 inches

from green

2 strips, each 2 × 65½ inches (top and bottom borders)

2 strips, each 2 × 84 inches (side borders)

2 strips, each 2 × 74½ inches (top and bottom borders)

2 strips, each 2 × 93 inches (side borders)

80 strips, each 2 × 14 inches

To make full blocks

See Figure 1.

1. With right sides facing, join a white lattice strip to the top edge of a floral square so you have 3½ inches of white fabric extending on each side. (This is to give you enough fabric to make the mitered corners. If corners will butt, cut off excess on each side edge.)

2. Press seam to one side

3. Repeat with another white lattice strip on the bottom edge of the square in the same way.

4. See Figure 2. With right sides facing, join a green lattice strip to each side edge of the floral square in the same way. Make 31 blocks in this way.

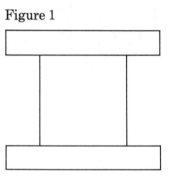

Figure 1

To make half blocks

1. With right sides facing, join a white lattice strip to one side of a floral triangle. Press seam to one side.

2. With right sides facing, join a green lattice strip to the other side edge in the same way. The lattice strips will meet where the extra fabric will be used to make the mitered corners. Make 18 in this way.

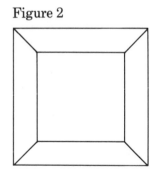

Figure 2

To make rows

Refer to Figure 3.

1. With right sides facing, join 2 half blocks so the white lattice strip of one is joined with the green lattice strip of the other to make row 1 as shown. Press seams to one side.

2. With right sides facing, join 2 full blocks, alternating

their positions so you have a green lattice strip from one block joined with a white lattice strip from the other.

3. With right sides facing, and again joining a white lattice strip to a green one and vice versa, join a half block to each end to make row 2 as shown.

4. Press seams to one side.

5. Refer to Figure 3 and continue to make 9 rows in this way, ending with 2 half blocks for row 9.

Figure 3

To join rows

Refer to Figure 4.

1. With right sides facing and seams aligned, join row 1 to row 2 along the bottom edge of row 1 and the top edge of row 2.

2. Press seam to one side.

3. Continue to join rows as shown. Press seams to one side.

Figure 4

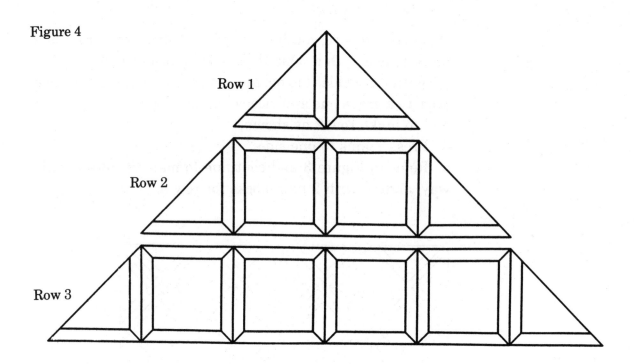

Row 1

Row 2

Row 3

To join borders

Refer to Figure 5.

1. With right sides facing, join the shortest white strips (2 × 62½ inches) to the top and bottom edges of the quilt top.

2. Press seams to one side.

3. Next, with right sides facing, join the 2-×-81-inch white strips to each side edge of the quilt top. Press seams to one side.

4. With right sides facing, join the shortest green strips (2 × 65½ inches) to the top and bottom edges of the quilt top. Press seams to one side.

5. With right sides facing, join the 2-×-84-inch green strips to each side edge of the quilt.

6. Press seams to one side.

7. Next, with right sides facing, join the shorter floral strips to the top and bottom edges of the quilt top.

8. Press seams to one side.

9. Repeat with the remaining floral strips on each side edge of the quilt.

10. With right sides facing, join the 2 × 74½ inch green strips to the top and bottom edges of the quilt top. Press seams to one side.

11. With right sides facing, join the remaining green strips to the side edges of the quilt top in the same way. Press seams to one side.

12. With right sides facing, join the 2×77 inch white strips to the top and bottom edges of the quilt top. Press seams to one side.

13. With right sides facing, join the remaining white strips to the side edges of the quilt top in the same way. Press seams to one side.

To prepare backing

1. Cut the backing fabric in half so you have 2 pieces, each 2¾ yards.

2. With right sides facing, join the 2 pieces along one side edge to make a backing piece to fit the quilt top. You will have extra fabric all around. Trim so you have approximately 3 inches all around.

To quilt

1. With wrong sides facing and batting between, pin the backing, batting, and quilt top together.

2. Beginning in the center and working outward in a sunburst pattern, take long, loose basting stitches through all three layers of material.

3. Take small running stitches ¼ inch from each side of all seam lines, stopping short of the seam allowance around the outside edge of the quilt.

To finish

1. When all quilting is complete, remove the basting stitches.

2. Trim the batting ¼ inch smaller than the quilt all around.

3. Trim the backing fabric to same size as the quilt top.

4. Turn the raw edges of the backing to the inside ¼ inch and press.

5. Turn the raw edges of the quilt top to the inside ¼ inch and press.

6. Matching stitch all around to finish.

Pinwheel Crib Quilt

The Pinwheel is a whimsical pattern for a baby's quilt. This is a quick-and-easy project and can also be used in the carriage, bassinet, or to carry along when traveling with baby. It's the perfect shower or baby gift and is inexpensive to make because it takes under four yards of fabric. The finished size is 37 × 54 inches. My daughter, Robby, made this quilt in colors that would be appropriate for a boy or girl, but you can substitute your own color combination.

Materials
(all fabric is 45 inches wide)
½ yard light green print
½ yard light blue print
¾ yard yellow
2 yards peach (includes backing)
1½ yards quilt batting
tracing paper
cardboard for template

Directions
Note: All measurements include ¼-inch seam allowance. Trace pattern A. This is half the pattern needed. You can pin to the fold of fabric or turn the tracing over on the center line and trace again to make the larger triangle. Transfer to cardboard for the template (see page 19). Cut out.

Cut the following:
from light blue
     A—12
from light green
     A—12
from yellow
     A—24
from peach

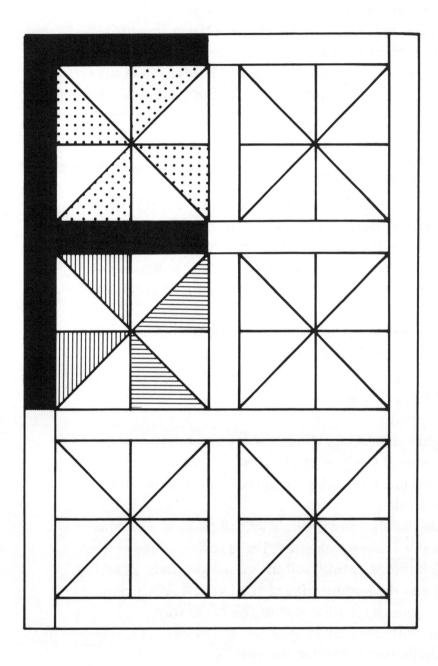

backing piece 37½ × 54½ inches
2 border strips, each 3½ × 54½ inches (sides)
4 lattice strips, each 3½ × 31½ inches
3 lattice strips, each 3½ × 14½ inches

Tip: To get the best use of your fabric, plan a layout on paper before cutting your fabric. This is especially helpful when you are cutting a backing piece and borders from the same fabric. You want to be sure to cut the largest piece first.

To make a block
Refer to Figure 1.

Figure 1

1. With right sides facing, stitch a blue triangle to a yellow triangle along the diagonal to make a square. Press seam to one side. Make 3 more squares in this way.
2. Refer to Figure 2. With right sides facing, stitch the 4 squares together to make a block as shown. Press seams to one side.
3. Make 3 blocks using the yellow-and-blue triangles and 3 blocks using the green-and-yellow triangles.

Figure 2

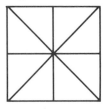

To assemble quilt top
Refer to Figure 3.

1. With right sides facing, stitch a short peach lattice strip to the right side of the blue block. Next, join this to the left side of a green block to make the top row of the quilt. Press seams to one side.
2. Alternate the blue and green blocks to make the middle and bottom rows in the same way. Press seams to one side.
3. With right sides facing, stitch one of the long peach lattice strips to the bottom edge of the top row. With right sides facing, join the middle row in the same way.
4. Continue with another long peach lattice strip to connect the middle row to the bottom row.
5. With right sides facing, stitch one of the remaining peach lattice strips to the top edge of the top row, and the other strip to the bottom edge of the bottom row. Press all seams to one side.

6. With right sides facing, stitch one peach border strip to each side of the quilt top. Press seams to one side.

To quilt

1. With wrong sides facing, pin the quilt top, batting, and backing together.

2. Begin at the center of the quilt and take long, loose basting stitches outward in a sunburst pattern through all three layers.

3. Using small running stitches, quilt ¼ inch from each side of all seam lines. Stop quilting stitches ½ inch from outer edges all around.

Figure 3

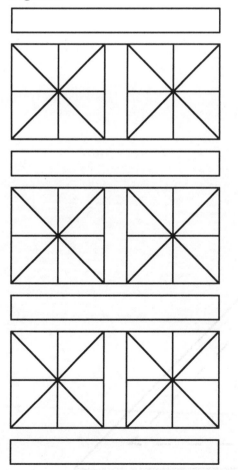

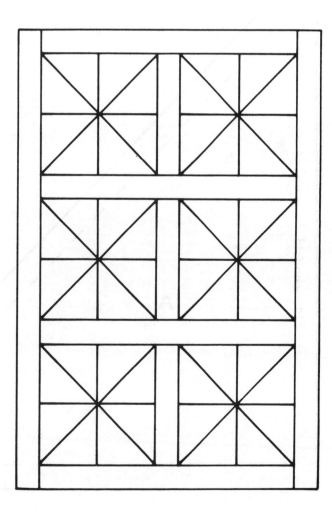

To finish

1. When all quilting is complete, remove basting stitches.
2. Trim batting ½ inch smaller than quilt top all around. Trim backing to the same size as the quilt top.
3. Turn the raw edges of the quilt top and backing to the inside ¼ inch all around and press.
4. Pin together and slipstitch or machine stitch close to the edge all around. Press.

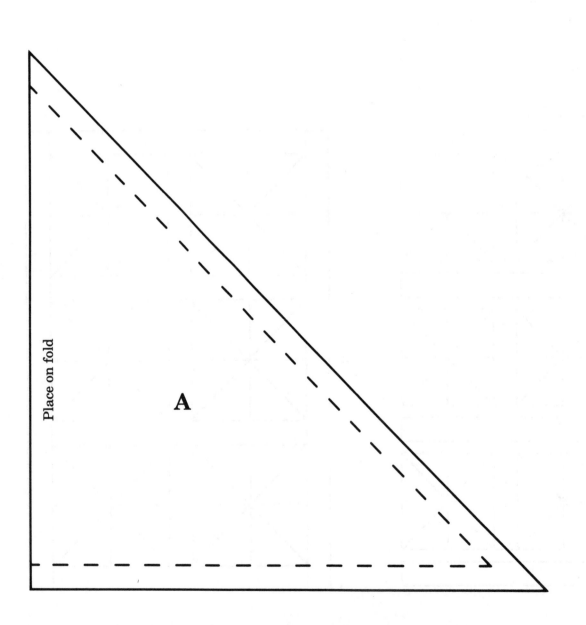

Place on fold

A

Pinwheel Pillows

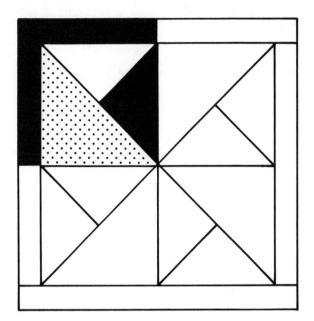

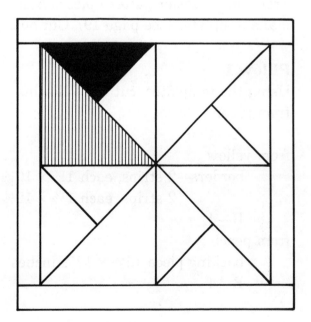

The Pinwheel pillows are perfect small quilting projects. While they match the Pinwheel quilt, each uses a slightly different color combination of the same fabrics. The finished size is 12×12 inches and can be filled with stuffing or a standard pillow form.

Materials

(for 2 pillows)
½ yard peach fabric
½ yard blue fabric
⅓ yard green fabric
⅓ yard yellow fabric
½ yard quilt batting
12-×-12-inch pillow forms or stuffing
49 inches cording for each pillow
tracing paper
cardboard for template

Directions

Note: All measurements include ¼-inch seam allowance. Trace and transfer pattern pieces A and B to cardboard to make templates (see page 19). Cut out.

Pillow 1

Using the templates, cut the following
from green
    A—4
from yellow
    borders—2 strips, each 1½ × 10½ inches
        2 strips, each 1½ × 12½ inches
    B—4
from peach
    backing piece 12½ × 12½ inches
    B—4

To assemble

Refer to Figure 1.
1. With right sides facing and raw edges aligned, join a yellow B piece to a peach B piece along one short edge to make a large triangle as shown.

Baby Bow Ties (page 28)

Lightning Streaks (page 33)

Friendship Ring (page 55)

Delectable Mountains (page 38)

Monkey Wrench (page 120)

Amish Square (page 63)

Sunshine Star Tablecover (page 71)

Singin' The Blues (page 113)

Baby Steps (page 128)

Christmas Throw (page 107)

Flying Kites (page 50)

Pinwheel Pillows (page 95)

Flannel Checkerboard (page 45)

Pinwheel Crib Quilt (page 90)

School Days (page 142)

Mini Irish Chain (page 136)

Kaleidoscope (page 152)

Pink Sails (page 76)

Patriotic Star (page 100)

Floral Frames (page 84)

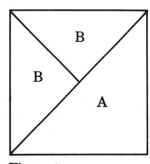

Figure 1

2. Press seam to one side.

3. Repeat with the remaining yellow B and peach B pieces.

4. With right sides facing and long edges aligned, join all yellow/peach triangles to the green triangle A pieces. Press seams to one side.

5. Refer to Figure 2 to join all 4 squares, making a small pinwheel in the center of the pillow top. Press seams to one side.

6. Next, add the borders in the following way: With right sides facing and raw edges aligned, attach a yellow 1½-×-10½-inch strip to one side edge of the block. Press seam to one side. Repeat on the opposite side.

7. Join the long strips to the top and bottom edges in the same way to complete the pillow top.

To quilt

1. Cut the quilt batting 11½ × 11½ inches and pin to the back of the pillow top.

2. Taking small running stitches, quilt ¼ inch from each side of all seam lines.

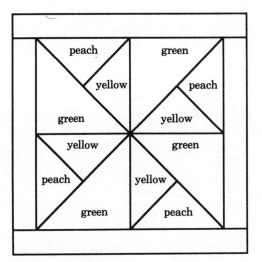

Figure 2   Pillow 1

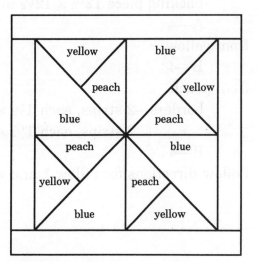

Figure 3   Pillow 2

To finish

1. Use any one of the fabrics to make a strip of fabric 1½ × 50 inches long for the piping to go around the pillow top. To do this, cut shorter strips of fabric on the bias and stitch the short ends of the strips together to make one long strip.

2. Beginning ½ inch from the end of the fabric, place the cording in the center of the wrong side of the fabric. Fold the fabric over the cording so the raw edges of the fabric meet.

3. Use a zipper foot on your sewing machine and stitch as close to the cording as possible to encase it in the fabric.

4. With right sides facing and raw edges aligned, pin the piping around the edge of the pillow top, overlapping the ends.

5. Stitch the piping to the pillow top as close to the cording as possible.

6. With right sides facing and raw edges aligned, stitch the backing piece to the pillow top, using the piping stitches as a guide and leaving 8 inches across one edge open for turning. Trim seams and clip corners.

7. Turn right side out and insert pillow form or stuffing. Slipstitch opening closed or insert a zipper according to package directions.

Pillow 2

Use the same templates and cut the following
from blue

  backing piece 12½ × 12½ inches

  A—4

from yellow

  B—4

from peach

  borders—2 strips, each 1½ × 10½ inches

      2 strips, each 1½ × 12½ inches

  B—4

Follow directions for pillow 1 and refer to Figure 3.

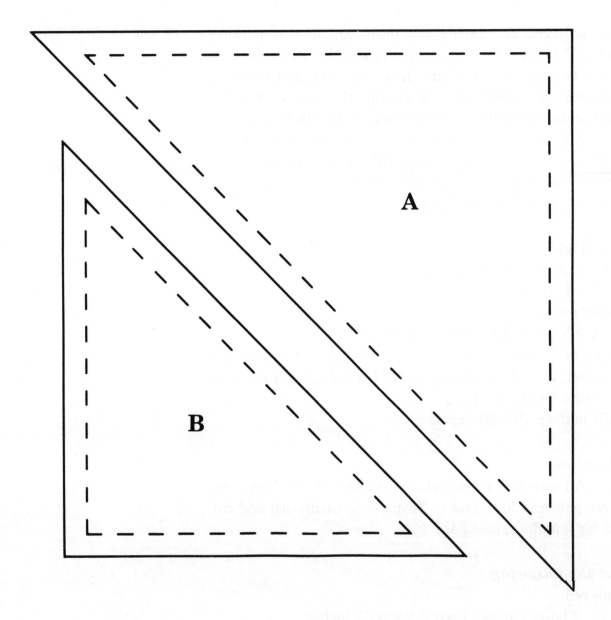

A

B

Patriotic Star

Star patterns are among the most popular for making quilts. This full-size quilt is a good example of a traditional use of two colors with white. It is very bold and exciting. However, you might want to change the colors, or use a combination of calico prints rather than solids as shown here. Although this quilt is a bit trickier than those made with straight stitching, it is not difficult, and once you've pieced one block it will be easy to make the rest. The finished size is 79 × 89 inches.

Materials
(all fabric is 45 inches wide)
2½ yards red fabric
3 yards blue fabric
8½ yards white fabric (includes backing)
Optional: For the backing you may use a flat double white sheet, in which case you will only need 3½ yards white fabric for the quilt top.
quilt batting 79 × 89 inches

Directions
Note: All measurements include a ¼-inch seam allowance. Trace patterns A, B, and C. Transfer to cardboard and cut out for templates (see page 19).

Cut the following
from red
      2 border strips, each 2½ × 80½ inches
      2 border strips, each 2½ × 66½ inches
      A—72 pieces
from blue
      2 border strips, each 2½ × 88½ inches
      2 border strips, each 2½ × 74½ inches
      B—96
      C—48 pieces

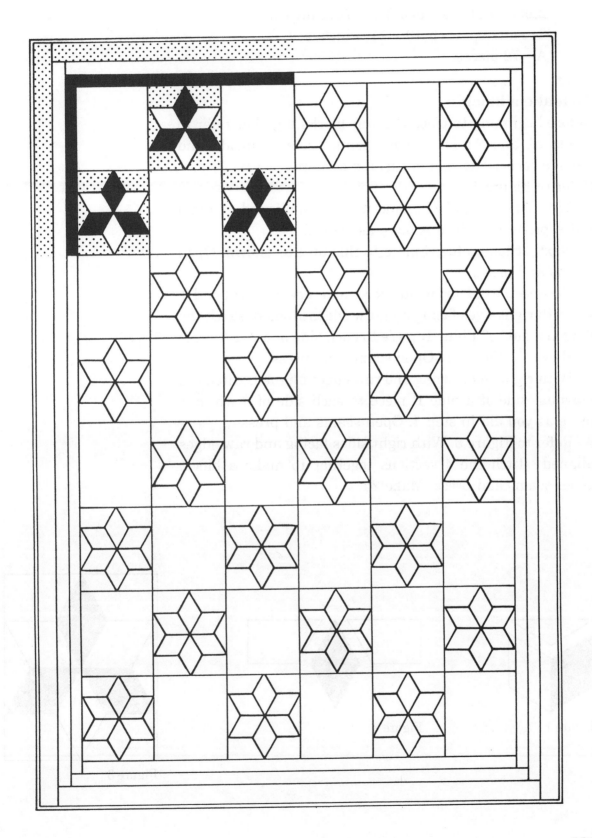

from white (cut backing pieces first)

        backing—2 pieces, each 45 × 91 inches
        2 border strips, each 2½ × 84½ inches
        2 border strips, each 2½ × 70½ inches
        24 squares, each 10 × 11½ inches
        A—72 pieces

To make a block

Before beginning to piece the star blocks together refer to pages 21 and 22 for sewing points, sewing inside and outside corner edges, and turning corners.

Refer to Figure 1.

1. With right sides facing and raw edges aligned, stitch a red A piece to a white A piece as shown.

2. Next, stitch a blue C piece to this unit as shown. Open seams and press.

3. Reverse the red and white pieces and repeat steps 1 and 2.

4. With right sides facing and raw edges aligned, stitch the diagonal side of a blue B piece to each side of a red A piece as shown in Figure 2. Open seams and press.

5. With right sides facing and raw edges aligned, stitch the diagonal side of a blue B piece to each side of a white A piece as you did in step 4. Open seams and press.

6. Refer to Figure 3. With right sides facing and raw edges aligned, stitch the 4 sections together to make a block. Open seams and press. Make 24.

Figure 1

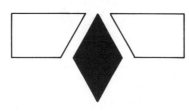

Figure 2

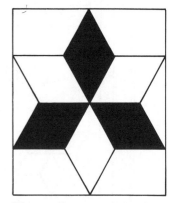

Figure 3

To make rows

Refer to Figure 4.

Row 1

1. With right sides facing and raw edges aligned, stitch a star block to a white square. Press seam to one side.

2. Continue to join another star block, a white square, another star block, and end the row with a white square to make a row of 3 star blocks separated by 3 white squares as shown. Make 4 rows in this way.

Row 2

1. With right sides facing and raw edges aligned, stitch a white square to a star block. Press seam to one side.

2. Continue with another white square, followed by another star block, a white square, and end with a star block to complete a row of 3 white squares separated by 3 star blocks. Make 4 rows in this way.

Figure 4

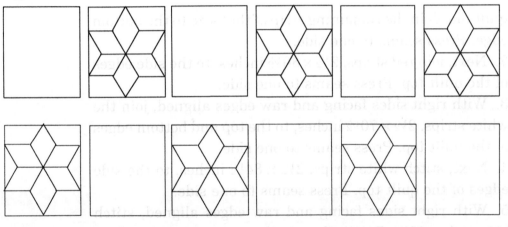

To join rows

Refer to Figure 5.

1. With right sides facing and raw edges aligned, join row 1 to the top edge of row 2. Press seam to one side.

2. Alternate row 1 with row 2 and continue to join all 8 rows in this way.

To join borders

1. With right sides facing and raw edges aligned, stitch a red border strip, 2½ × 66½ inches, to the top edge of the

Figure 5

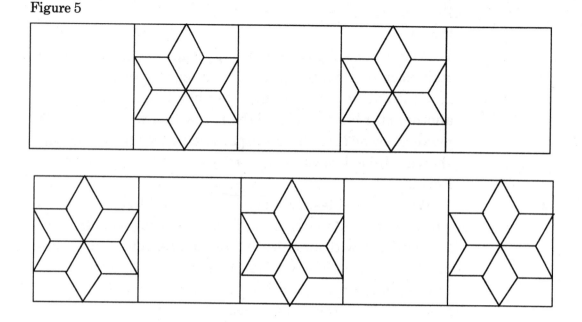

quilt top. Join the remaining strip of that size to the bottom edge. Press seams to one side.

2. Next, join red strips, 2½ × 80½ inches, to the side edges of the quilt top. Press seams to one side.

3. With right sides facing and raw edges aligned, join the white strips, 2½ × 70½ inches, to the top and bottom edges of the quilt top. Press seams to one side.

4. Next, stitch white strips, 2½ × 84½ inches, to the side edges of the quilt top. Press seams to one side.

5. With right sides facing and raw edges aligned, stitch blue strips, 2½ × 74½ inches, to the top and bottom edges of the quilt top.

6. Next, stitch blue strips, 2½ × 88⅛ inches, to the side edges of the quilt top. Press seams to one side.

Preparing the backing
Refer to page 19 for directions on transferring quilting patterns.

1. Trace and transfer the quilting pattern to each star block and to each white square.

2. With right sides facing, stitch the 2 backing pieces together to make a piece 90 × 91 inches.

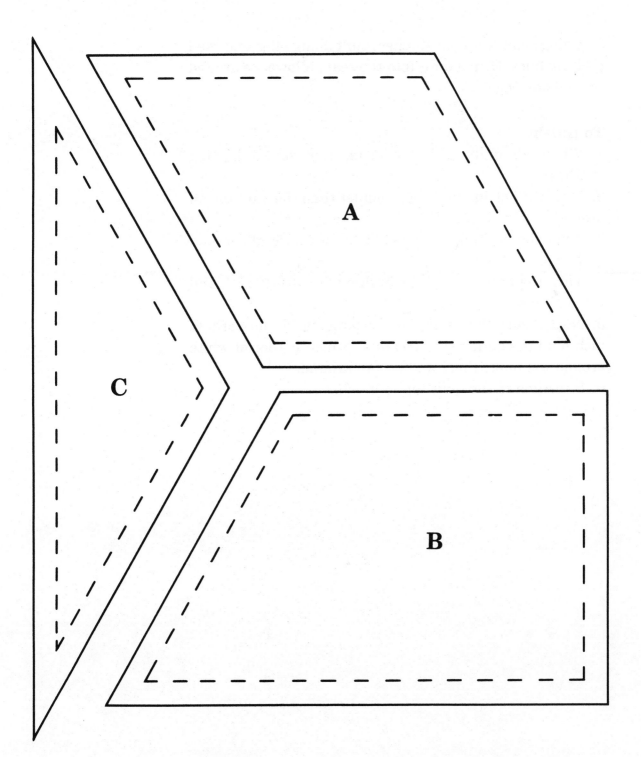

To quilt

1. With wrong sides facing and batting between, pin backing, batting, and quilt top together. There will be extra backing fabric all around.

2. Starting at the center of the top and working outward in a sunburst pattern, baste all three layers together with long, loose stitches.

3. Using small running stitches, quilt along all premarked quilting lines. Do not quilt into the seam allowance around the outside edge.

To finish

1. When all quilting is complete, remove all basting stitches.

2. Trim the batting to ½ inch smaller than the quilt top all around.

3. Trim the backing, leaving 1 inch of fabric all around quilt top.

4. Turn the raw edges of the backing forward ½ inch and press all around.

5. Next, bring the remaining backing fabric forward ½ inch onto the quilt top to create a ½-inch border of white around the quilt. Press and pin all around.

6. Slipstitch to the quilt top to finish.

Christmas Throw

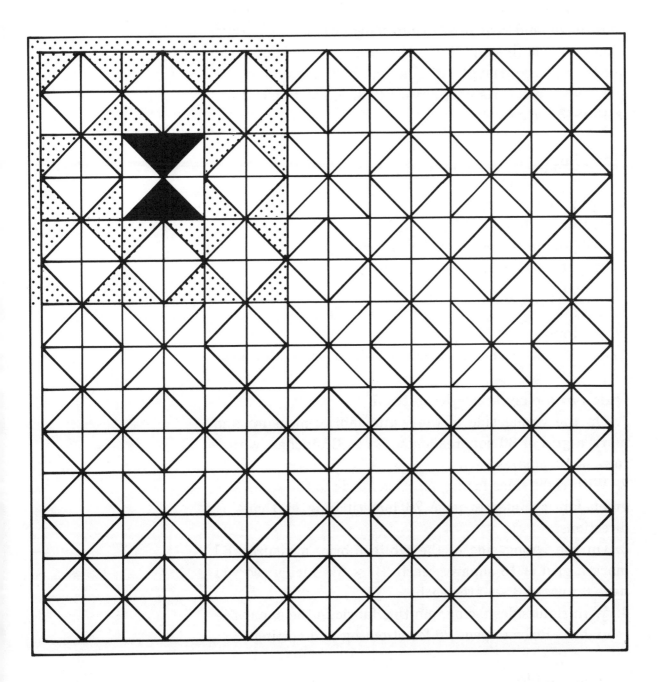

It's always fun to make a quilted wallhanging for the holidays. Star patterns are among the most popular, and you can make this one with the red, white, and green print as shown here for the holidays, or choose colors to match your room and use it all year long. My mother, Ruth Linsley, made this and it was the first time she'd used the quick-and-easy triangle piecing method. Now she says she'll never piece triangles any other way. The finished size is 43 × 43 inches.

Materials
(all fabric is 45 inches wide)
1 yard green print fabric
1½ yards white fabric
2 yards red print fabric (includes backing)
quilt batting 45 × 45 inches
quilt marker

Directions
Note: All measurements include a ¼-inch seam allowance.

Quick-and-easy triangle method
1. On the wrong side of the white fabric, measure and mark a grid of 80 squares, each 3⅞ × 3⅞ inches, with 8 rows of 10 squares each.
2. With right sides facing, pin this fabric to the same size green fabric. Refer to page 26 for stitching and cutting directions.
3. On the wrong side of the white fabric, measure and mark a grid of 18 squares, each 3⅞ × 3⅞ inches, so you have 6 rows of 3 squares each.
4. With right sides facing, pin this fabric to the same size red fabric. Refer to page 26 for stitching and cutting.

To make a block
Refer to Figure 1 to arrange rows of green/white squares and red/white squares.

1. With right sides facing, join 4 green/white squares to make row 1 as shown. Press seams to one side.

2. Next, join a white/green square to a red/white square along the right-side edge as shown, followed by another red/white square and ending row 2 with a green/white square. Press seams to one side.

3. With right sides facing, join a white/green square to a red/white square, followed by another red/white square and ending row 3 with a green/white square. Press seams to one side.

4. With right sides facing, join 4 green/white squares as shown to make row 4. Press seams to one side.

5. With right sides facing and seams aligned, join the rows to make a block as shown in Figure 2. Make 9 blocks in this way.

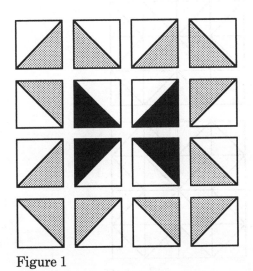

Figure 1

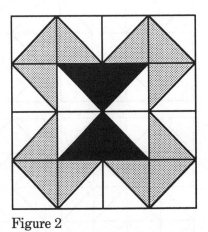

Figure 2

To piece borders

Refer to Figure 3.

1. To make side borders: With right sides facing, join a green/white square to another green/white square along one edge as shown. Press seam to one side.

2. Continue to join 12 squares in this way. Make 2.

3. To make top and bottom borders: With right sides facing, join a green/white square to another green/white square along one edge as shown. Press seam to one side.

4. Continue to join 14 squares in this way. Make 2.

Figure 3

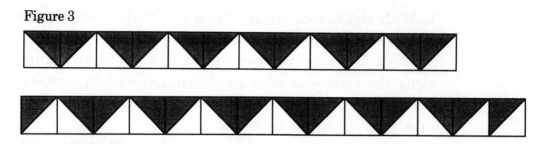

To join blocks

Refer to Figure 4.

1. With right sides facing, join 2 blocks along the right-side edge. Press seam to one side.

2. Next, join another block in the same way to make a row of 3 blocks.

3. Press seam to one side. Make 3 rows in this way.

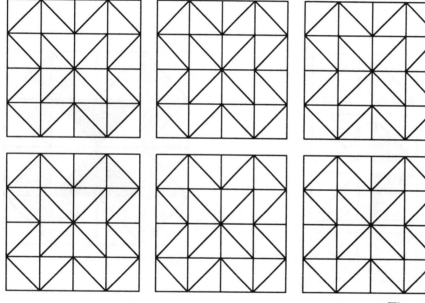

Figure 4

To join rows

Refer to Figure 5.

1. With right sides facing and seams aligned, join the bottom edge of the first row to the top edge of the second row.

2. Press seam to one side.

3. Join the last row in the same way.

To join borders

Refer again to Figure 6.

1. With right sides facing, join a side border strip to the left-side edge of the quilt top as shown.

110

2. Press seam to one side.

3. Repeat on the opposite side edge.

4. With right sides facing, join a top border strip to the top edge of the quilt as shown.

5. Press seam to one side.

6. Repeat on the bottom edge of the quilt top with the remaining border strip.

Figure 5

To quilt

1. With wrong sides facing and batting between, pin the backing, batting, and quilt top together.

2. Beginning at the center of the quilt and working outward in a sunburst pattern, take long, loose basting stitches through all three layers, stopping short of the seam allowance around the outside edges.

3. Take small running stitches ¼ inch from each side of all seam lines, stopping short of the seam allowance around the quilt top.

To finish

1. When all quilting is complete, remove basting stitches.
2. Trim the batting ¼ inch smaller than quilt top all around.
3. Next, turn the raw edges of the backing forward ¼ inch and press.
4. Bring the remaining backing fabric forward to bind the edges of the quilt top and press. Pin all around and slipstitch to finish the quilt.

Figure 6

Singin' the Blues

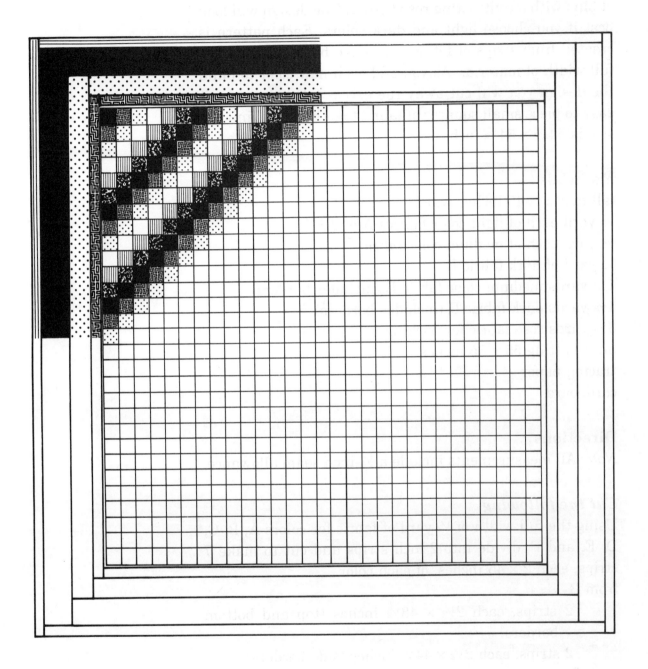

Make this project to hang on the wall or to use as a lap throw on chilly evenings. Kate McCombe based this quilt design on 1½-inch squares and combined different shades of blue with a contrasting rose border. The design will look best if you choose light and dark colors. Each pattern is created from strips of fabric that have been cut from the full width of material. As you add each new color to build the design you will cut away the excess fabric to make it easy to piece small squares of fabric together. The finished size is 54½ × 54½ inches.

Materials
(all fabric is 45 inches wide)
½ yard each of light color fabrics A and F
½ yard each of medium color fabric C
½ yard of dark fabric E
1½ yards medium color fabric B (includes borders)
1⅔ yards dark fabric D (includes borders)
3⅓ yards rose fabric for backing
quilt batting 55 × 55 inches
tracing paper
cardboard

Directions
Note: All measurements include a ¼-inch seam allowance.

Cut the following
Using the full width of ½ yard of fabric for colors A, B, C, D, E, and F, divide into 2-inch strips and cut to make 7 strips, each 2 × 45 inches, of each color.
from B
> 2 strips, each 2½ × 48½ inches (top and bottom borders)
>
> 2 strips, each 2½ × 44½ inches (side borders)

from D
> 2 strips, each 2½ × 53½ inches (top and bottom borders)
>
> 2 strips, each 2½ × 49½ inches (side borders)

from E

   2 strips, each 1 × 44½ inches (top and bottom
   borders)

   2 strips, each 1 × 43½ inches (side borders)

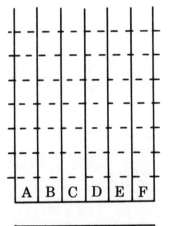

Figure 1a

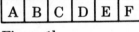

Figure 1b

To make pieced strips

Refer to Figure 1a.

1. With right sides facing, join an A strip to a B strip along one long edge.

2. Press seam to one side.

3. Next, with right sides facing, join a C strip to the B strip along the raw edge in the same way. Press seam to one side.

4. Continue to add the D strip, then an E strip and an F strip. Press seams to one side. Make 7 units in this way.

5. Next, refer to Figure 1b and mark across each unit at 2-inch intervals. Cut apart to make 140 pieced strips (you'll need only 136, but it's best to have a few extras).

To make rows for upper right section

Refer to Figure 2.

1. Starting with the bottom row and with right sides facing, join 2 pieced strips along one short end to make a longer strip as shown.

2. Press seam to one side. Next, add another strip in the same way. Take a third strip and pull the stitches out between the C and D squares and set aside the D, E, F piece to be used in row 4.

3. Follow the chart and continue to make rows using the pieced strips in this way.

To join rows

1. With right sides facing and seams aligned, join row 1 and row 2.

2. Press seam to one side.

3. Continue to join rows in this way, making sure all color sequences are accurate as shown in Figure 2.

4. Press seams to one side.

To make rows for upper left section

Refer to Figure 3.

1. Separate the A, B, C section from the D, E, F section of a pieced strip and with right sides facing, join them along the short end of the A and F squares.

2. Press seam to one side.

3. Continue to join pieced squares according to the chart to make 15 rows in this way.

To join rows

1. With right sides facing and seams aligned, join row 1 with row 2 along the long edge as shown in Figure 3.

2. Press seam to one side.

3. Continue to join rows in this way as you did for the upper right section.

To make lower left section

Refer to Figure 4 to make rows, and join rows to complete this section of the quilt as you did for the upper sections.

To make lower right section

Refer to Figure 5 to make rows, and join rows to complete this section of the quilt as you did for the other sections.

To join sections

Refer to Figure 6.

1. With right sides facing and seams aligned, join the upper left section and the upper right section along the right-side edge.

2. Press seam to one side.

3. With right sides facing and seams aligned, join the lower left section and the lower right section along the right-side edge.

4. Press seam to one side.

5. With right sides facing and seams aligned, join the top and bottom pieces along the long edge to complete the pieced top.

6. Press seam to one side.

Upper left grid:

C	B	A	F	E	D	C	B	A	F	E	D	C	B
D	C	B	A	F	E	D	C	B	A	F	E	D	C
E	D	C	B	A	F	E	D	C	B	A	F	E	D
F	E	D	C	B	A	F	E	D	C	B	A	F	E
A	F	E	D	C	B	A	F	E	D	C	B	A	F
B	A	F	E	D	C	B	A	F	E	D	C	B	A
C	B	A	F	E	D	C	B	A	F	E	D	C	B
D	C	B	A	F	E	D	C	B	A	F	E	D	C
E	D	C	B	A	F	E	D	C	B	A	F	E	D
F	E	D	C	B	A	F	E	D	C	B	A	F	E
A	F	E	D	C	B	A	F	E	D	C	B	A	F
B	A	F	E	D	C	B	A	F	E	D	C	B	A
C	B	A	F	E	D	C	B	A	F	E	D	C	B
D	C	B	A	F	E	D	C	B	A	F	E	D	C
E	D	C	B	A	F	E	D	C	B	A	F	E	D

Upper right grid:

A	B	C	D	E	F	A	B	C	D	E	F	A	B	C
B	C	D	E	F	A	B	C	D	E	F	A	B	C	D
C	D	E	F	A	B	C	D	E	F	A	B	C	D	E
D	E	F	A	B	C	D	E	F	A	B	C	D	E	F
E	F	A	B	C	D	E	F	A	B	C	D	E	F	A
F	A	B	C	D	E	F	A	B	C	D	E	F	A	B
A	B	C	D	E	F	A	B	C	D	E	F	A	B	C
B	C	D	E	F	A	B	C	D	E	F	A	B	C	D
C	D	E	F	A	B	C	D	E	F	A	B	C	D	E
D	E	F	A	B	C	D	E	F	A	B	C	D	E	F
E	F	A	B	C	D	E	F	A	B	C	D	E	F	A
F	A	B	C	D	E	F	A	B	C	D	E	F	A	B
A	B	C	D	E	F	A	B	C	D	E	F	A	B	C
B	C	D	E	F	A	B	C	D	E	F	A	B	C	D
C	D	E	F	A	B	C	D	E	F	A	B	C	D	E

Lower left grid:

E	D	C	B	A	F	E	D	C	B	A	F	E	D
D	C	B	A	F	E	D	C	B	A	F	E	D	C
C	B	A	F	E	D	C	B	A	F	E	D	C	B
B	A	F	E	D	C	B	A	F	E	D	C	B	A
A	F	E	D	C	B	A	F	E	D	C	B	A	F
F	E	D	C	B	A	F	E	D	C	B	A	F	E
E	D	C	B	A	F	E	D	C	B	A	F	E	D
D	C	B	A	F	E	D	C	B	A	F	E	D	C
C	B	A	F	E	D	C	B	A	F	E	D	C	B
B	A	F	E	D	C	B	A	F	E	D	C	B	A
A	F	E	D	C	B	A	F	E	D	C	B	A	F
F	E	D	C	B	A	F	E	D	C	B	A	F	E
E	D	C	B	A	F	E	D	C	B	A	F	E	D
D	C	B	A	F	E	D	C	B	A	F	E	D	C

Lower right grid:

C	D	E	F	A	B	C	D	E	F	A	B	C	D	E
B	C	D	E	F	A	B	C	D	E	F	A	B	C	D
A	B	C	D	E	F	A	B	C	D	E	F	A	B	C
F	A	B	C	D	E	F	A	B	C	D	E	F	A	B
E	F	A	B	C	D	E	F	A	B	C	D	E	F	A
D	E	F	A	B	C	D	E	F	A	B	C	D	E	F
C	D	E	F	A	B	C	D	E	F	A	B	C	D	E
B	C	D	E	F	A	B	C	D	E	F	A	B	C	D
A	B	C	D	E	F	A	B	C	D	E	F	A	B	C
F	A	B	C	D	E	F	A	B	C	D	E	F	A	B
E	F	A	B	C	D	E	F	A	B	C	D	E	F	A
D	E	F	A	B	C	D	E	F	A	B	C	D	E	F
C	D	E	F	A	B	C	D	E	F	A	B	C	D	E
B	C	D	E	F	A	B	C	D	E	F	A	B	C	D

Figure 5

Upper left section	Upper right section

Lower left section	Lower right section

Figure 6

To make borders

Refer to Figure 7.

1. With right sides facing, join a short E border strip to one side edge of the pieced top.

2. Press seam to one side.

3. Repeat with the other short E strip on the opposite side edge in the same way.

4. With right sides facing, join the remaining E strips to the top and bottom edges of the quilt in the same way.

5. Press seams to one side.

6. With right sides facing, join the short B border strips to each side edge of the quilt in the same way.

7. With right sides facing, join the remaining B border strips to the top and bottom edges of the quilt in the same way.

8. With right sides facing, join the side D border strips to each side edge in the same way.

9. Join remaining D strips to the top and bottom edges of the quilt top in the same way.

10. Press all seams to one side.

To prepare backing

1. Cut the rose backing fabric in half to create 2 pieces, each 45 × 60 inches.

2. With right sides facing, join the 2 pieces along one long side edge to create a backing piece 60 × 90 inches.

3. Trim this piece to 60 inches square. (The excess might be used to make a pillow.)

To quilt

1. With wrong sides facing and batting between, pin the backing, batting, and top together. There will be excess backing fabric all around the edges.

2. Starting at the center and working outward in a sunburst pattern, take long, loose basting stitches through all three layers.

3. Take small running stitches on each side of the inside border seam lines. If you want to quilt the entire top, take small running stitches on each side of all seam lines. Do not stitch into the seam allowance around the outside edges.

118

To finish

1. Turn the raw edges of the quilt top under ¼ inch and press all around.

2. Trim the backing fabric so it's 1½ inches larger than the quilt top all around.

3. Fold the raw edges of the backing forward ¼ inch and press.

4. Bring the remaining fabric forward to encase the raw edges of the quilt top and pin to the front of the quilt. Press.

5. Slipstitch all around to complete the wallhanging.

Figure 7

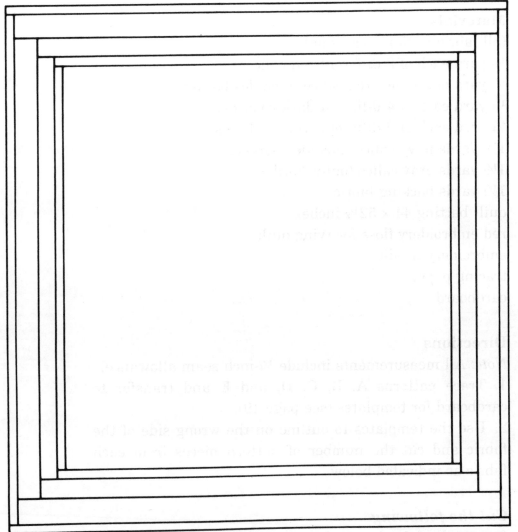

Monkey Wrench

This quilt pattern has been adapted by Kate McCombe of Nantucket Island. Kate has a wonderful sense of color and has selected a variety of up-to-date pretty prints that look both traditional yet new at the same time. The quilt could be used as a throw over a sofa for chilly evenings, on a single bed, or as a wallhanging. The finished size is 44 × 52½ inches. To make it larger, simply add another border all around.

Materials
(all fabric is 45 inches wide)
⅛ yard each of 3 different red calicoes
¼ yard of another red calico (includes border)
¼ yard each of 4 different dark color calicoes
¼ yard each of 2 different white calicoes
1½ yards navy calico (includes border)
1½ yards gray calico (outer border)
1½ yards backing fabric
quilt batting 44 × 52½ inches
red embroidery floss for tying quilt
embroidery needle
tracing paper
cardboard

Directions
Note: All measurements include ¼-inch seam allowance.
1. Trace patterns A, B, C, D, and E and transfer to cardboard for templates (see page 19).
2. Use the templates to outline on the wrong side of the fabric and cut the number of pattern pieces from each fabric as indicated below.

Cut the following
from each of the 4 red calicoes
      5 strips, each 1½ × 10 inches (a total of 20 strips)

from red calico (¼ yard)

    2 strips, each 1½ × 34½ inches

    2 strips, each 1½ × 45 inches

from each of the dark calicoes

    A—20 (80 pieces total)

    B—5 (20 pieces total)

from each of the white calicoes

    A—40 (80 pieces total)

    10 strips, each 1½ × 10 inches (a total of 20 strips)

from navy calico

    C—12

    D—11

    E—4

    borders—2 strips, each 3½ × 36½ inches

            2 strips, each 3½ × 51 inches

from gray calico

    borders—2 strips, each 1½ × 42½ inches

            2 strips, each 1½ × 53 inches

To make a block

See Figure 1a.

1. With right sides facing, stitch a dark calico A piece to a white calico A piece to make a square. Press seam to one side. Use the same color combination to make 4 squares in this way.

2. Using the same color white calico, with right sides facing, stitch a 1½-x-10-inch strip to a same size red calico strip along one long edge. Press seam to dark side. Make 20 units.

3. Refer to Figure 1b. Measure and cut the sewn strip into 2½-inch units. Make 4 units.

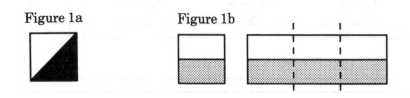

Figure 1a   Figure 1b

4. Arrange the 4 squares, 4 units, and one dark calico B piece into 3 rows according to Figure 2a.

5. With right sides facing, stitch the 3 pieces together to make each row. Press seams to one side.

6. Refer to Figure 2b. With right sides facing, stitch the bottom edge of the top row to the top edge of the middle row. Next, join the bottom row in the same way to make a block. Press seams to one side. Make 20 blocks in this way. The A piece and the B square should be the same color for each block.

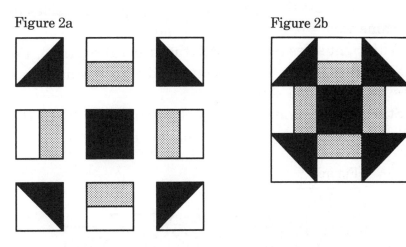

Figure 2a   Figure 2b

To make rows

Refer to Figure 3. *Note:* this quilt is set on the diagonal.

1. Arrange the blocks with the navy C squares, D large triangles, and E small triangles into 8 rows according to Figure 3.

2. With right sides facing, stitch one short side of a navy D piece to the left side of a block. Then stitch the right side of the block to the short side of another navy D piece to make row 1. Stitch the long edge of an E piece to the top edge of the block. Press seams to one side.

3. Continue to join blocks and C, D, and E pieces to make all 8 rows according to the layout. Press seams to one side.

To join rows

1. With right sides facing, stitch the bottom edge of row 1 to the top edge of row 2. Press seam to one side.

2. Continue to join all 8 rows in this way to make the quilt top. Press seams to one side.

To add borders

Refer to Figure 4.

1. With right sides facing, stitch one red calico strip, 1½ × 34½ inches, to the top edge and another to the bottom edge of the quilt top. Press seams to one side.

2. Next, stitch the remaining 2 red calico strips to the sides in the same way.

3. With right sides facing, stitch the navy calico strips, 3½ × 36½ inches, to the top and bottom edges of the quilt top. Press seams to one side.

4. Stitch the remaining 2 navy calico strips to the sides in the same way. Press seams to one side.

5. With right sides facing, stitch the gray calico strips, 1½ × 42½ inches, to the top and bottom edges of the quilt top. Press seams to one side.

6. Stitch the remaining 2 gray strips to the sides of the quilt in the same way. Press seams to one side.

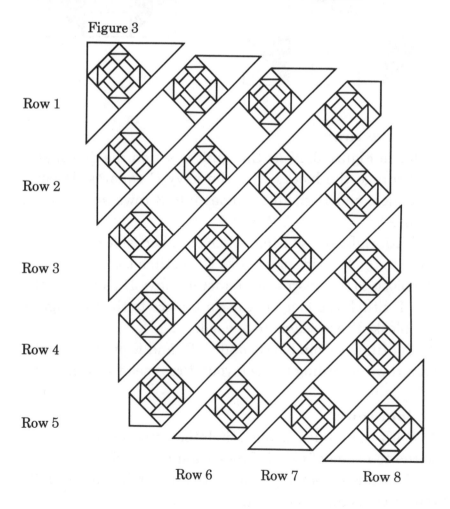

Figure 3

Row 1

Row 2

Row 3

Row 4

Row 5

Row 6   Row 7   Row 8

To quilt

1. With wrong sides facing, pin the quilt top, batting, and backing together.

2. Beginning at the center and taking long, loose stitches, baste through all three layers together.

3. Tie the quilt at each corner of each block in the following way: cut 8-inch lengths of embroidery floss. Thread your embroidery needle and, working from the top, insert the needle through the three layers, then back up again close to the first stitch. Remove the needle, tie the floss in a knot, and cut the ends to within ½ inch.

To finish

1. After you've tied the quilt, remove all basting stitches.

2. Trim the batting ½ inch smaller than the quilt top all around.

3. Trim the backing fabric to the same size as the quilt top.

4. Turn the raw edges of the quilt top and backing fabric to the inside ¼ inch all around and press.

5. Slipstitch edges together.

Figure 4

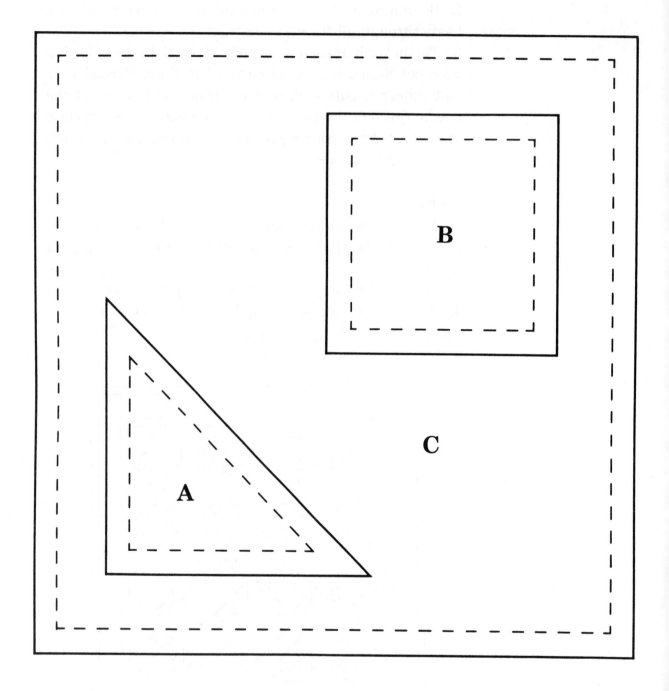

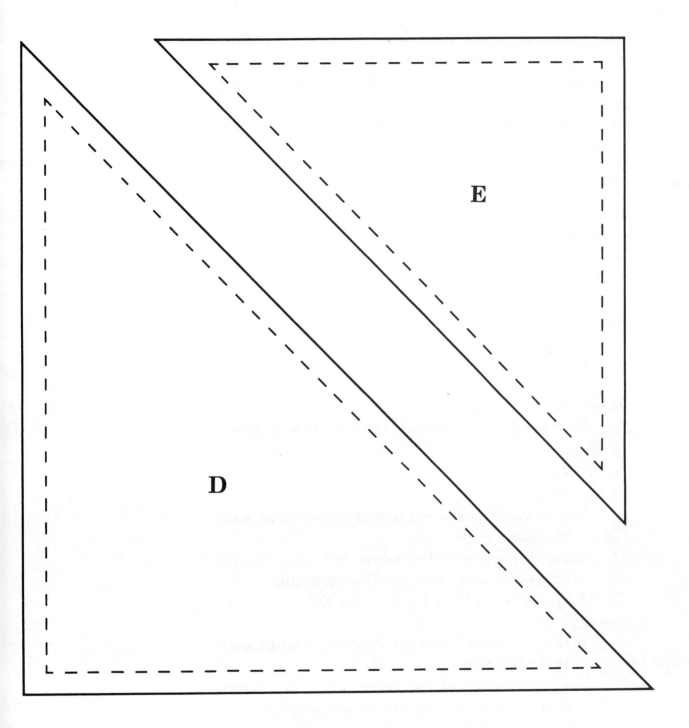

E

D

Baby Steps

Peter Peluso, Jr., chose a simple color combination of two shades of pink and two shades of blue to make a baby quilt. The pattern is made from 1¼-inch squares, and the strip piecing method is used for ease of piecing. The blue borders are connected with 4 squares, 3 blue and 1 pink, in each corner. The finished size is 34¼ × 43¼ inches, and you can make a matching pillow if desired.

Materials

(all fabric is 45 inches wide)
¾ yard white fabric (A)
½ yard light blue fabric (B)
½ yard pale pink fabric (C)
½ yard rose fabric (D)
2 yards dark blue fabric (E)
quilt batting 35 × 44 inches

Directions

Note: All measurements include ¼-inch seam allowance.

Cut the following

from white (A)

      border (cut from full width of fabric), 4 strips, each 1¾ inches wide

      using full width of the fabric, cut into 1¾-inch strips—cut each strip into 12-inch lengths

      8 squares, each 1¾ × 1¾ (for corners)

from light blue (B)

      border (cut from full width of fabric), 4 strips, each 1¾ inches wide

      using full width of the fabric, cut into 1¾-inch strips—cut each strip into 12-inch lengths

      4 squares, each 1¾ × 1¾ inches (for corners)

from pale pink (C)

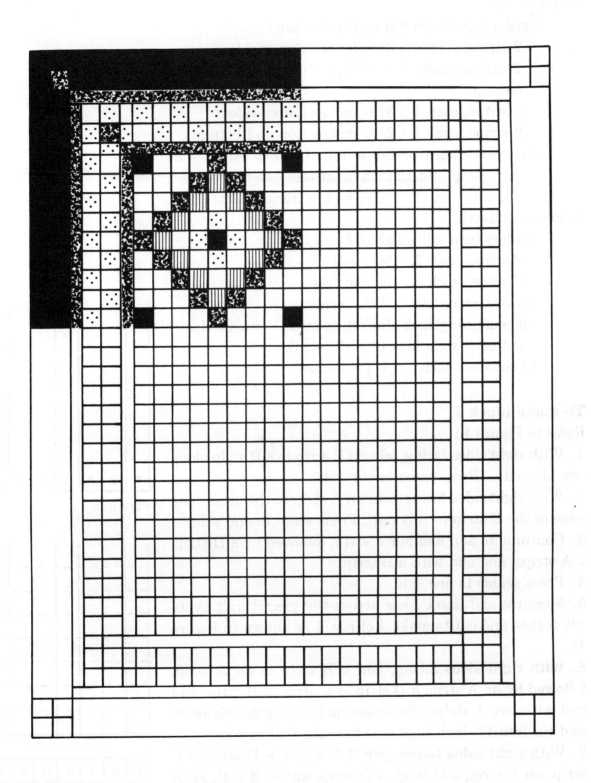

using full width of the fabric, cut into 1¾-inch strips—cut each strip into 12-inch lengths

from rose (D)

borders (cut from full width of fabric)

2 strips, each 1 × 31¾ inches (inner sides)

2 strips, each 1 × 22¾ inches (inner top and bottom)

2 strips, each 1 × 37¾ inches (outer sides)

2 strips, each 1 × 29¾ inches (top and bottom)

cut remaining rose fabric into 1¾-inch strips—cut each strip into 12-inch lengths

8 squares, each 1¾ × 1¾ inches (for corners)

from dark blue (E)

borders (use full width of fabric)

2 strips, each 3 × 38¾ inches

2 strips, each 3 × 34¾ inches

backing piece 34¾ × 43¾ inches

cut remaining dark blue fabric into 1¾-inch strips— cut each strip into 12-inch lengths

12 squares, each 1¾ × 1¾ inches

To make block 1

Refer to Figure 1a.

1. With right sides facing, join an E strip to a B strip along one long edge. Press seam to one side.

2. With right sides facing, join an A strip to the other long edge of the B strip in this unit. Press seam to one side.

3. Continue to add another A strip, followed by a D strip, 2 A strips, and end with a B strip.

4. Press seams to one side.

5. Measure and mark lines across the pieced unit every 1¾ inches and cut to make 4 of row 1 as shown in Figure 1b.

6. With right sides facing, join a B strip to an A strip, followed by an A strip, a D strip, a C strip, a D strip, and end with two A strips. Press seams to one side. Measure and cut into 1¾ inch segments to make 6 of row 2.

7. With right sides facing, join 2 A strips, a D strip, a C strip, an A strip, a C strip, a D strip, and end with an A

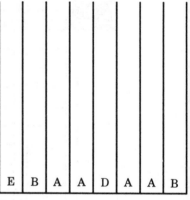

| E | B | A | A | D | A | A | B |

Figure 1a

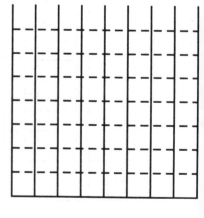

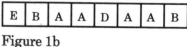

| E | B | A | A | D | A | A | B |

Figure 1b

130

strip. Press seams to one side. Cut into 1¾-inch segments to make 6 of row 3.

8. With right sides facing, join an A strip to a D strip along one side edge. Press seam to one side. Continue to add strips C, A, B, A, C, and D in this way. Measure and cut into 1¾-inch segments to make 6 of row 4.

9. With right sides facing, join a D strip to a C strip, followed by strips A, B, E, B, A, and C in the same way. Press seams to one side.

10. Measure and cut into 1¾-inch segments to make 3 of row 5 (rows 6 and 7 are the same as rows 4 and 3).

11. With right sides facing, join 3 A strips, a D strip, a C strip, a D strip, 2 A strips. Measure and cut into 1¾-inch segments to make 3 of row 8.

12. Refer to Figure 1c. With right sides facing and seams aligned, join rows 1 and 2. Press seam to one side.

13. Continue to add rows 3 through 5 in the same way.

14. Rows 6 and 7 are the same as rows 4 and 3. Join these rows.

15. Next add row 8 in the same way to complete block 1. Make 3 of block 1.

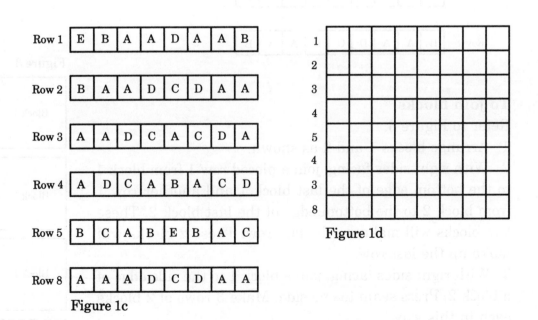

| Row 1 | E | B | A | A | D | A | A | B |

| Row 2 | B | A | A | D | C | D | A | A |

| Row 3 | A | A | D | C | A | C | D | A |

| Row 4 | A | D | C | A | B | A | C | D |

| Row 5 | B | C | A | B | E | B | A | C |

| Row 8 | A | A | A | D | C | D | A | A |

Figure 1c

Figure 1d

To make block 2

Refer to Figure 2a.

1. Join strips of fabric and cut into segments for block 2 as for block 1 in the following sequences:

Row 1 (make 4)—E, B, A, A, D, A, A, B, E

Row 2 (make 6)—B, A, A, D, C, D, A, A, B

Row 3 (make 6)—A, A, D, C, A, C, D, A, A

Row 4 (make 6)—A, D, C, A, B, A, C, D, A

Row 5 (make 3)—D, C, A, B, E, B, A, C, D

Row 8 (make 3)—B, A, A, D, C, D, A, A, B

2. Refer to Figure 2b to join rows for block 2 as you did to make block 1. Make 3 of block 2.

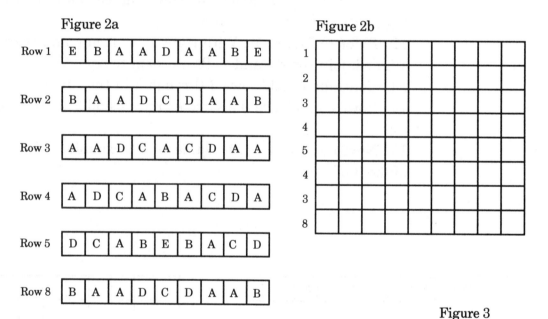

Figure 2a

Row 1 | E | B | A | A | D | A | A | B | E
Row 2 | B | A | A | D | C | D | A | A | B
Row 3 | A | A | D | C | A | C | D | A | A
Row 4 | A | D | C | A | B | A | C | D | A
Row 5 | D | C | A | B | E | B | A | C | D
Row 8 | B | A | A | D | C | D | A | A | B

Figure 2b

To join blocks

Refer to Figure 3.

1. Arrange blocks 1 and 2 as shown.

2. With right sides facing, join a pieced row 1 from block 1 to the bottom edge of the last block 1 and another row 1 from block 2 to the bottom edge of the last block 2. These two blocks will make up the last row. These 2 blocks will make up the last row.

3. With right sides facing, join a block 1 to the side edge of a block 2. Press seam to one side. Make 3 rows of 2 blocks each in this way.

4. With right sides facing, join all 6 blocks.

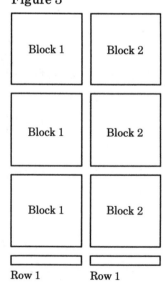

Figure 3

Block 1	Block 2
Block 1	Block 2
Block 1	Block 2

Row 1   Row 1

132

To make checkerboard borders

1. With right sides facing, join a 45-inch long white (A) and a 45-inch long light blue (B) strip along one side edge. Make 4.
2. Press seam to one side.
3. Measure and cut into 1¾-inch segments.
4. With right sides facing and alternating the blue and white segments to create a checkerboard pattern, join 18 pieced segments to create the top border strip.
5. Repeat for the bottom border.
6. Piece together 26 blue-and-white segments to make the side border strips in the same way. Make 2.

Figure 4a

B	A
A	D

To make patchwork corners

Refer to Figure 4a.
1. With right sides facing, join a white (A) 1¾-inch square to a pale blue (B) square. Press seam to one side.
2. Next, join a rose (D) 1¾-inch square to a white (A) square of the same size. Press seam to one side.
3. With right sides facing, join the 2 rows as shown. Make 2 corners in this way.
4. Refer to Figure 4b. Join a pale blue (B) square to one side edge of a rose (D) square.
5. Join an A square to a B square in the same way.

Figure 4b

B	D
A	B

6. With right sides facing, join the 2 rows as shown. Make 2 corners in this way.
7. With right sides facing, join 2 pale blue (B) 1¾ inch squares. Press seams to one side.
8. Next, join a pale blue (B) square along one side edge of a rose (D) square.
9. With right sides facing, join these 2 rows to make a corner square. Make 4.
10. Refer to Figure 5 for placement of patchwork corners. With right sides facing, join the blue/white/rose corners to each end of the side checkerboard strips. Press seams to one side.
11. With right sides facing, join the blue-and-white patchwork corners to the short ends of each long, 3-x-38¾-inch dark blue (E) side border strips. Press seams to one side.

To join borders

Refer to Figure 5.

1. With right sides facing, join a rose (D) border strip, 1 ×
31¾ inches, to each side edge of the pieced quilt top.
2. Press seams to one side.

Figure 5

3. Repeat with the rose (D) border strips, $1 \times 22\frac{3}{4}$ inches, to the top and bottom edges of the pieced quilt top. Press seams to one side.

4. Next, with right sides facing, join a short checkerboard border strip to the top and bottom edges of the quilt top. Press seams to one side.

5. Repeat with the long checkerboard strips (with patchwork corners) to each side edge of the quilt top. Press seams to one side.

6. Next, with right sides facing, join a rose (D) border strip, $1 \times 29\frac{3}{4}$ inches, to the top and bottom edges of the quilt top in the same way.

7. With right sides facing, join a dark blue (E) border strip, $3 \times 34\frac{3}{4}$ inches, to the top edge of the quilt top. Press seams to one side.

8. Repeat on the bottom edge in the same way.

9. With right sides facing, join the long, dark blue border strips (with patchwork corners) to each side edge of the quilt. Press seams to one side.

To finish

Since the patches are so small on this quilt, the seam lines are close enough together that it doesn't require hand quilting. However, if you'd like to add quilting to make it more special, you can refer to any of the other quilts for directions on hand quilting.

1. With wrong sides facing and batting between, pin backing, batting, and top together.

2. Beginning at the center and working outward in a sunburst pattern, take long, loose basting stitches through all three layers.

3. To hold layers together permanently, machine stitch along seam lines of each corner square and around the 2 dark blue center squares.

4. Trim the batting ¼ inch smaller than the quilt top all around.

5. Trim the backing fabric to same size as the quilt top.

6. Turn the backing fabric ¼ inch to the inside and press.

7. Turn the top fabric to the inside ¼ inch and press. Pin together all around.

8. Machine stitch all around to finish.

Mini Irish Chain

If you've already made a bed-size quilt, it's fun to make a small wallhanging for a change of pace. Kate McCombe says once you make a small quilt you'll never want to make a full quilt again. Made with the strip piecing method (see page 25), this project is quick and easy and small enough to take with you for quilting-on-the-go.

The little wallhanging is 37 × 37 inches, and the pattern is called a Double Irish Chain. It's a variation on the traditional Irish Chain pattern often used by early American quilters. If you have fabric leftover from a bed quilt, it can be used to make this delightful project to hang on the wall over the bed.

Materials
(all fabric is 45 inches wide)
2 yards white calico fabric (includes backing), A
½ yard green calico fabric, B
½ yard brown calico fabric, C
quilt batting 37 × 37 inches
Velcro tabs for hanging

Directions
Note: All measurements include a ¼-inch seam allowance.

Cut the Following
from white A
        borders—2 strips, each 1 × 33½ inches (top and bottom)
                2 strips, each 1 × 43½ inches (sides)
        for block 1—1 strip 5 × 36 inches
                8 rectangles 5 × 8 inches
        for block 2—2 strips, each 2 × 20 inches
                1 strip 2 × 36 inches
        backing piece 38 × 38 inches
from green B

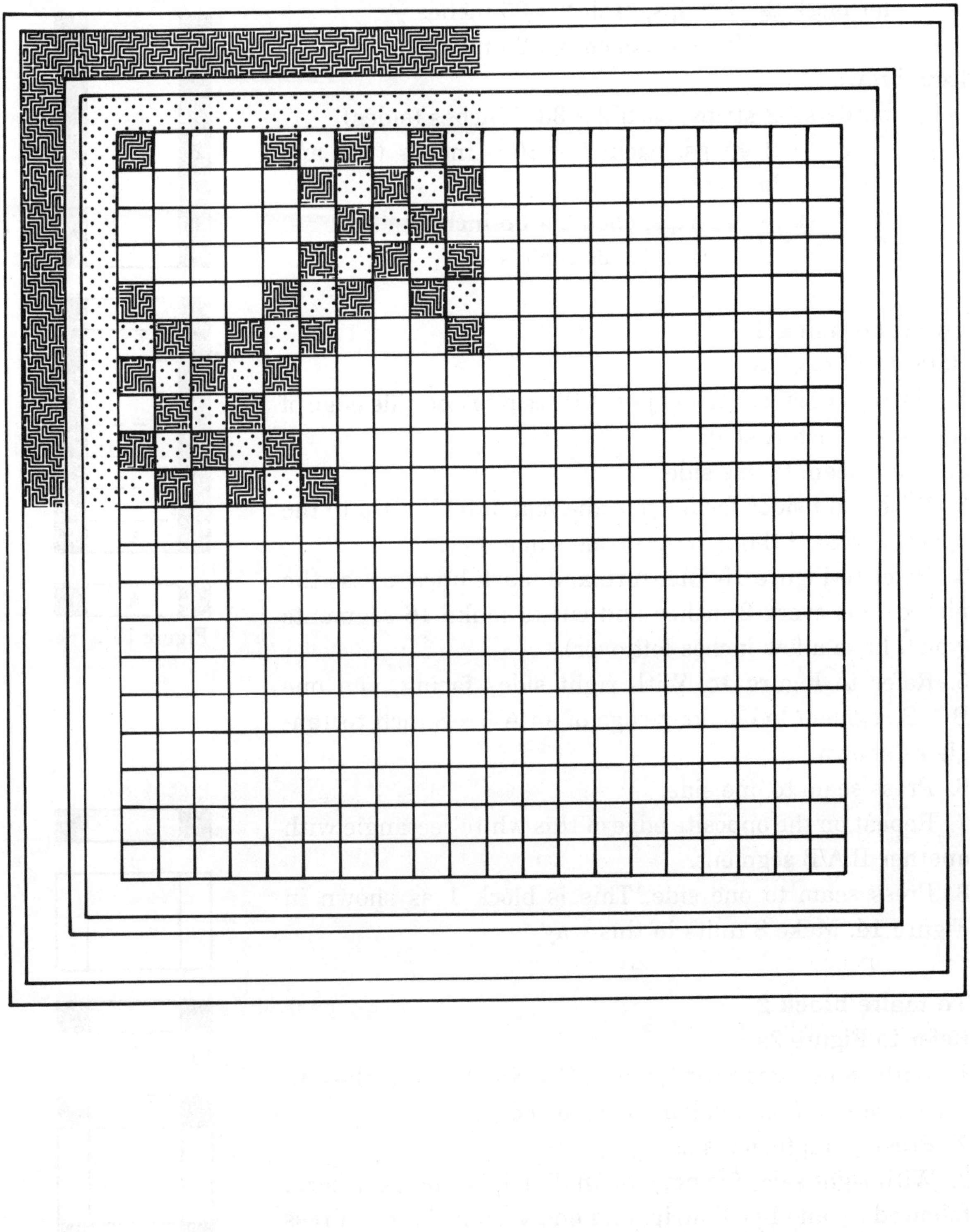

borders—2 strips, each 2 × 37½ inches (top and bottom)

2 strips, each 2 × 34½ inches (sides)

for block 1—2 strips, each 2 × 36 inches

for block 2—5 strips, each 2 × 36 inches

2 strips, each 2 × 20 inches

from brown C

borders—2 strips, each 2 × 33½ inches (sides)

2 strips, each 2 × 30½ inches (top and bottom)

for block 2—4 strips, each 2 × 36 inches

1 strip 2 × 20 inches

Figure 1a

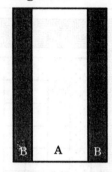

To make block 1
Refer to Figure 1a.

1. With right sides facing, join a B strip to one side edge of the 5-×-36-inch A strip.

2. Press seam to one side.

3. With right sides facing, join the matching B strip to the opposite side of the A strip in the same way.

4. Refer to Figure 1b. Measure and mark lines across the pieced unit every 2 inches and cut to make 16 segments (you'll have a few inches left over).

5. Refer to Figure 1c. With right sides facing, join one B/A/B segment to one long edge of an A 5-×-8-inch rectangle as shown.

6. Press seam to one side.

7. Repeat on the opposite edge of this white rectangle with another B/A/B segment.

8. Press seam to one side. This is block 1 as shown in Figure 1d. Make 8 units in this way.

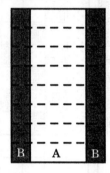

Figure 1b

To make block 2
Refer to Figure 2a.

1. With right sides facing, join a C strip, 2 × 36 inches, to the same size B strip along one side edge.

2. Press seam to one side.

3. With right sides facing, join an A strip of the same size, followed by another B strip, and end with a C strip. Press seams to one side.

Figure 1c

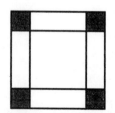

Figure 1d Block 1

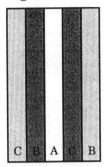
Figure 2a

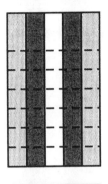

Figure 2b

4. Refer to Figure 2b. Measure and mark across the pieced unit every 2 inches and cut to get 16 segments (you'll have a few inches left over).

5. Next, with right sides facing, join a B strip (2 × 36 inches) to a C strip, to a B strip then a C strip, and end with a B strip. Measure and mark every 2 inches to get 16 segments.

6. Next, with right sides facing, join an A strip (2 × 20 inches) to a B strip of the same size. Press seam to one side.

7. With right sides facing, join a C strip (2 × 20 inches) to this unit, followed by another B strip, and end with another A strip.

8. Press seams to one side.

9. Measure and mark across this pieced unit every 2 inches and cut to get 8 segments.

10. Refer to Figure 2c to join rows. With right sides facing and seams aligned, join row 1 and row 2, followed by row 3. Press seams to one side.

11. Refer to Figure 2d and, with right sides facing, join row 4 (which is the same as row 2) and row 5 (which is the same as row 1). Press seams to one side. Make 8 blocks in this way.

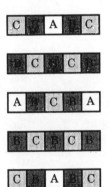

Figure 2c

To make a row

Refer to Figure 3.

1. With right sides facing, join a block 1 with a block 2 along the right-side edge.

2. Press seam to one side.

3. Next join a block 1 to the opposite side of block 2. Press seam to one side.

4. Finish the row by joining a block 2 in the same way. Make 2 rows in this way for rows 1 and 3.

To join rows

Refer to Figure 4.

1. With right sides facing and seams aligned, join row 1 with row 2. Press seam to one side.

2. Next, join row 3 to row 2 followed by row 4 in the same way.

3. Press seam to one side.

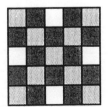

Figure 2d Block 2

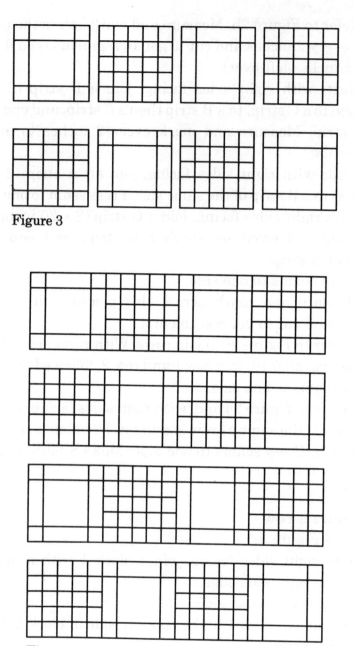

Figure 3

Figure 4

To join borders

1. With right sides facing, join a brown C border strip, 2 × 30½ inches, to the top edge of the pieced top.

2. Press seam to one side.

3. Repeat on the bottom edge in the same way.

4. Next, with right sides facing, join the 2-×-33½-inch

140

brown C strips to each side edge of the pieced top. Press seams to one side.

5. With right sides facing, join the 1-×-33½-inch white A strips to the top and bottom edges of the pieced top in the same way.

6. With right sides facing, join the remaining white A strips to the side edges of the pieced top. Press seams to one side.

7. With right sides facing, join a 2-×-34½-inch green B strip to the top edge of the quilt. Press seam to one side.

8. Repeat on the bottom edge in the same way.

9. With right sides facing, join the remaining green border strips to each side edge in the same way.

To quilt

1. With wrong sides facing and batting between, pin the backing, batting, and top together. There will be extra backing fabric all around.

2. Beginning in the center and working outward in a sunburst pattern, take long, loose basting stitches through all three layers.

3. Take small running stitches ⅛ inch from each side of all seam lines, stopping short of the seam allowance around the outside edges.

To finish

1. When all quilting is complete, remove basting stitches.

2. Fold the raw edges of the backing fabric forward ¼ inch and press.

3. Bring the remaining fabric forward to cover the raw edges of the quilt top and pin all around.

4. Slipstitch to finish.

To hang

Since this quilt is small and light, the easiest way to hang it is with Velcro tabs. Attach a tab to the back of the fabric at each corner and place another in the center of the top edge. Attach corresponding tabs to the wall where it will hang. Place in position. (For alternative ways to hang a quilt, see page 160.)

School Days

This lively rendition of the traditional Schoolhouse pattern was created with bright calico by Nancy Moore. Early quiltmakers often rendered this design by using red to symbolize the little red schoolhouse on a background of green or white calico. The use of these bright colors gives the design a different look suggesting bright, sunny school-days. There are 15 blocks. Use a different print for each block or make 2 or 3 blocks from the same fabric. The large patchwork makes it easy to assemble for a finished quilt measuring 60½ × 93½ inches.

Materials
(all fabric is 45 inches wide)
⅛ yard calico print for each of the 15 blocks (if 2 blocks are made of the same print you'll need ¼ yard of that print)
1 yard solid yellow fabric
2½ yards white or muslin fabric
2½ yards yellow calico (for borders)
5¼ yards backing fabric
quilt batting 62 × 95 inches
tracing paper
cardboard

Directions
Note: All measurements include a ¼-inch seam allowance. Trace patterns A through K and transfer to cardboard for templates (see page 19). Cut out.

Cut the following
For each of the 15 blocks:
from calico

A—2		H—1	
E—1		I—1	
F—1		J—2	
G—2		K—2	

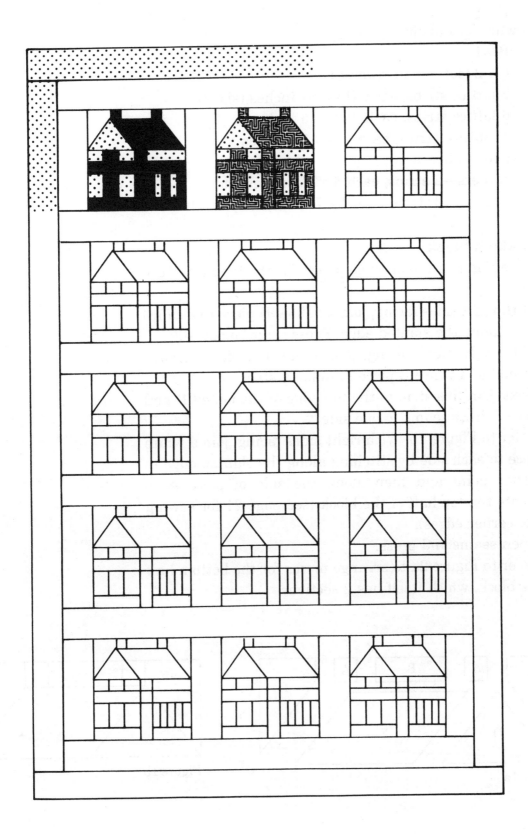

from solid yellow

        D—1   J—1
        F—2   K—3
        H—2
from white or muslin

        B—1
        C—2 (cut one in reverse)
        2 lattice strips, each 4½ × 87 inches (sides)
        6 lattice strips, each 4½ × 46 inches
        10 lattice strips, each 4½ × 13 inches
from yellow calico

        borders—2 strips, each 4 × 87 inches (sides)
                2 strips, each 4 × 70 inches (top and bottom)

To make a block

Refer to Figure 1a to arrange pieces for the top half of the block.

1. With right sides facing, join a yellow D piece to a calico E piece along the slanted edge. Press seam to one side.

2. With right sides facing, join a calico A piece to each short end of a white B piece to make a strip.

3. Next, join this strip to the top edge of the joined D and E pieces. Press seams to one side.

4. Refer to Figure 1b. With right sides facing, join a white C piece to each side by stitching along the slanted edge to a corner point and then along the side of piece A to complete the top half of the block (see page 21 for sewing inside corner edges).

5. Open seams and press.

6. Refer to Figure 2a to arrange pieces for the bottom half of the block, which itself has 2 sections.

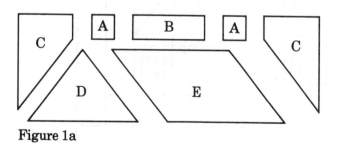

Figure 1a

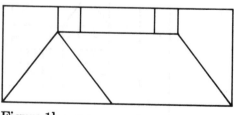

Figure 1b

144

Section 1

Refer to Figure 2b.

1. With right sides facing, join the short edge of a yellow F piece to each short edge of a calico F piece to make a strip as shown. Press seams to one side.

2. Next, with right sides facing, join a calico G piece to the bottom edge of this pieced strip. Press seam to one side.

3. With right sides facing, join a yellow H piece to each long side edge of a calico H piece as shown. Then, with right sides facing, join to the bottom edge of the calico G piece. Press seams to one side.

4. Next, join another calico G piece to the bottom edge of the joined H pieces made in step 3 to complete section 1 of the bottom half of the block.

5. With right sides facing, stitch a calico I piece to the right-side edge of section 1. Press seam to one side.

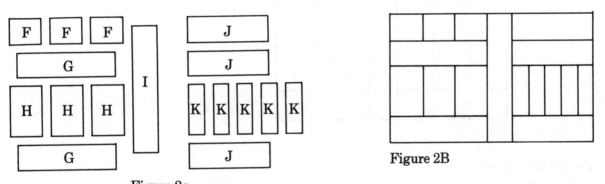

Figure 2a

Figure 2B

Section 2

Refer again to Figure 2b.

1. With right sides facing, join a calico J piece to the bottom long edge of a yellow J piece. Press seam to one side.

2. With right sides facing, join a yellow K piece to a calico K piece along the long edge. Then join another yellow K piece, followed by another calico K piece, followed by another yellow K piece as shown. Press seams to one side.

3. Next, join this pieced K section to the bottom edge of the calico J piece made in step 1.

145

4. With right sides facing, join another calico J piece to the bottom edge of the K section to complete section 2 of the bottom half of the block.

5. Press seams to one side.

6. With right sides facing, join section 2 to the raw side edge of the calico I piece to complete the bottom half of the block as shown.

7. Refer to Figure 3. With right sides facing, join the bottom edge of the top half of the block to the top edge of the bottom half of the block to complete the Schoolhouse block. Make 15 blocks in this way.

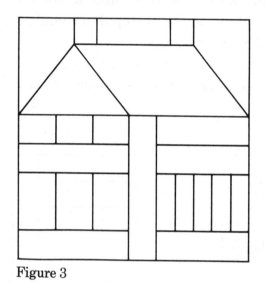

Figure 3

To make rows

Refer to Figure 4.

1. With right sides facing, join a block to the long edge of a short white lattice strip, 4½ × 13 inches.

2. Press seam to one side.

3. Next, with right sides facing, join this strip to another block along the side edge, then join the block to the long

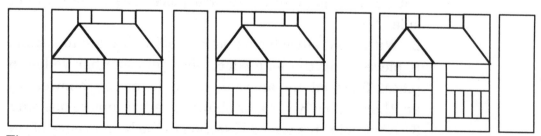

Figure 4

146

side edge of another lattice strip, followed by another block to make a row of 3 blocks separated by 2 short white lattice strips as shown.

4. Press all seams to one side. Make 5 rows in this way.

To join rows

Refer to Figure 5.

1. With right sides facing, join a white lattice strip, 4½ × 46 inches, to the top edge of row 1.

2. With right sides facing, join another white lattice strip to the bottom edge of row 1.

3. Continue to join all 5 rows, separated by a lattice strip and ending with a lattice strip at the bottom edge of the last row.

4. Press all seams to one side.

5. With right sides facing, join the remaining 2 lattice strips to each side edge of the quilt top as shown. Press seams to one side.

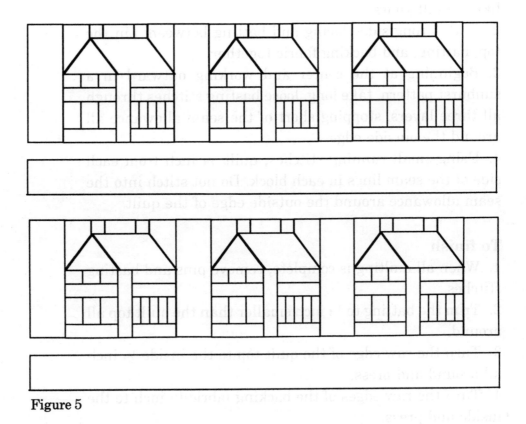

Figure 5

To add borders

1. With right sides facing, join a long yellow calico border strip to one side edge of the quilt top. Repeat on the opposite side and press seams to one side.

2. Next, join the remaining 2 yellow calico border strips to the top and bottom edges of the quilt top.

3. Press seams to one side.

To prepare backing

1. Cut the backing fabric in half lengthwise to make 2 pieces, each 45 × 94 inches. From one of these pieces cut 2 panels, each 9 × 94 inches.

2. With right sides facing, join a panel to each long side edge of the center backing piece to make one piece 62 × 94 inches. Press seams to one side.

To quilt

1. While this quilt has no hand stitching on it, you might like to quilt yours.

2. With wrong sides facing and batting between, pin the top, batting, and backing fabric together.

3. Beginning at the center and working outward in a sunburst pattern, take long, loose basting stitches through all three layers, stopping short of the seam allowance all around the outside edge.

4. Using small running stitches, quilt ¼ inch from each side of the seam lines in each block. Do not stitch into the seam allowance around the outside edge of the quilt.

To finish

1. When all quilting is complete, remove pins and basting stitches.

2. Trim the batting to ¼ inch smaller than the quilt top all around.

3. Turn the raw edge of the quilt top to the inside ¼ inch all around and press.

4. Turn the raw edges of the backing fabric ¼ inch to the inside and press.

5. Slipstitch or machine stitch along each edge of the quilt to complete.

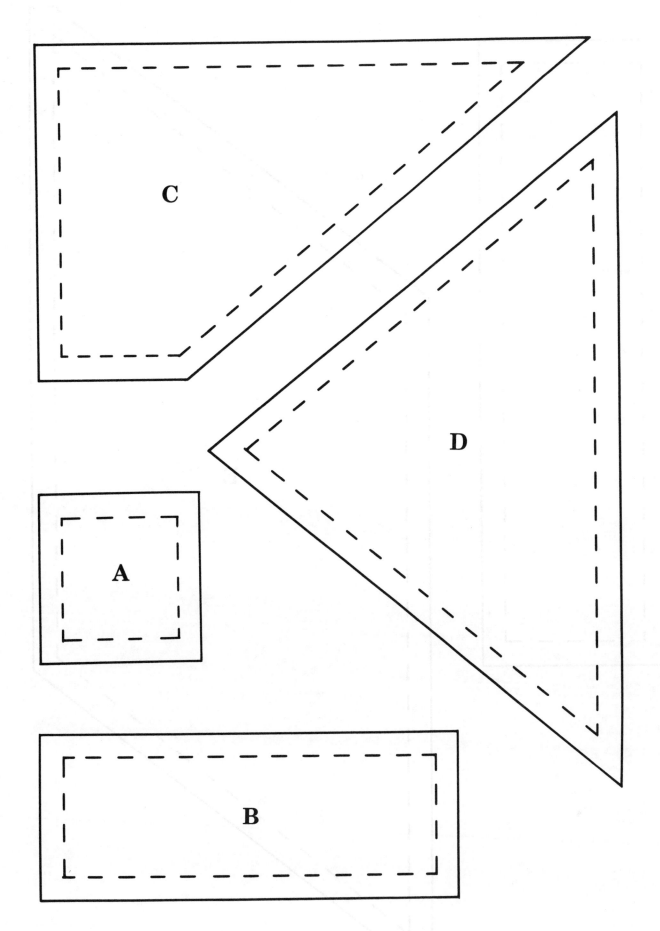

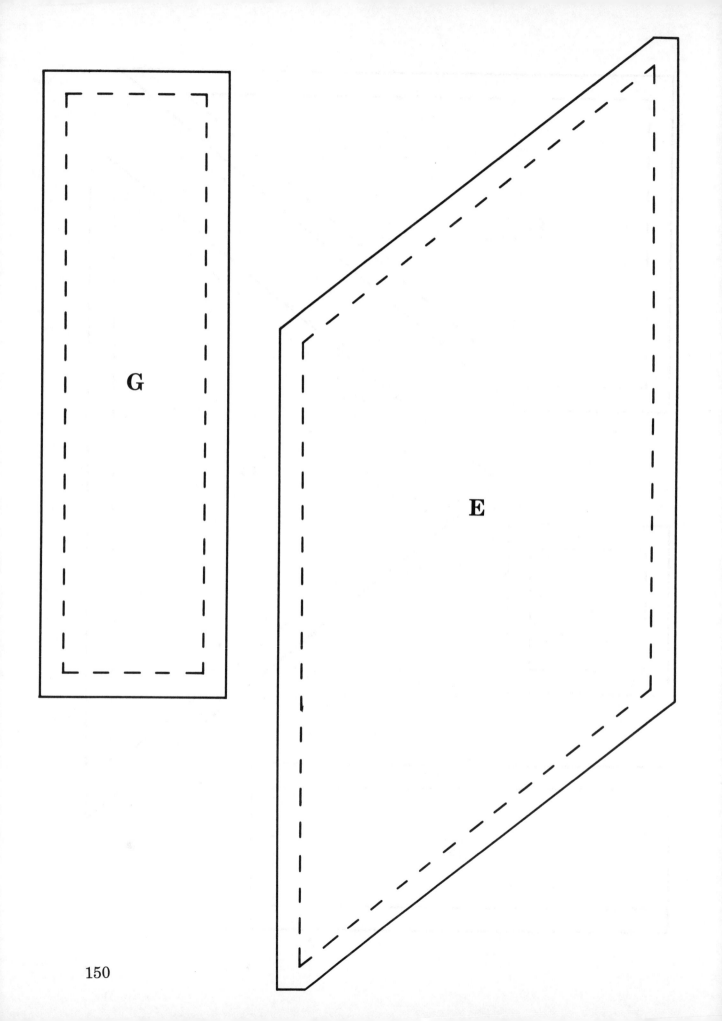

G

E

150

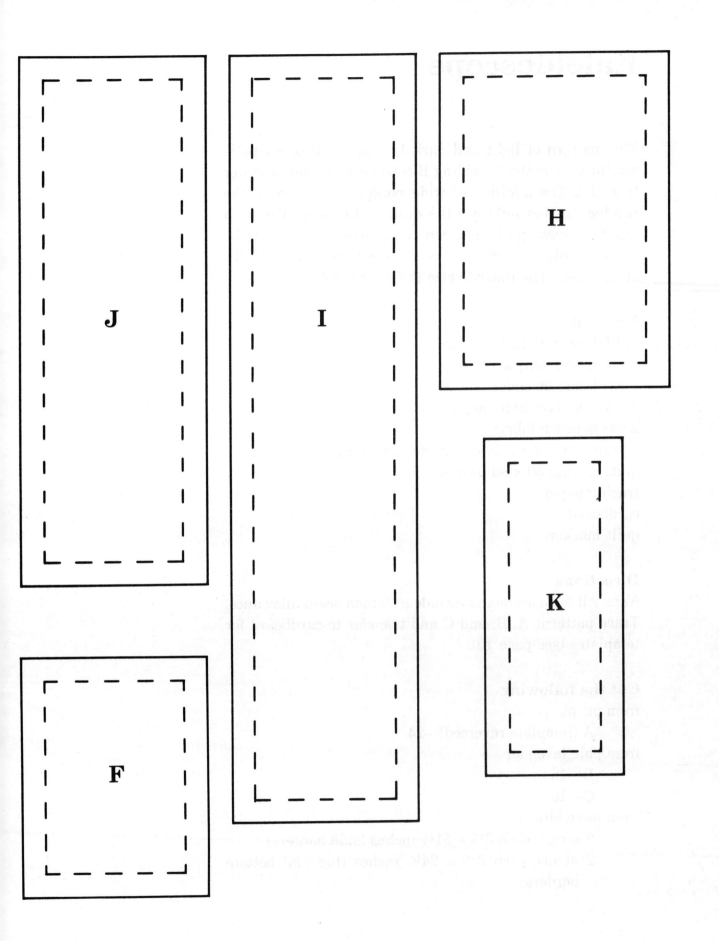

Kaleidoscope

This pattern of light and dark lavender lattice strips is reminiscent of the Tumbling Blocks pattern, but is easier to make. The addition of wide borders surrounding the patchwork area enlarges the quilt to full size. This is a quick-and-easy quilt that can be enlarged to any size by adding borders in different colors or light and dark shades of one color. The finished size is 60 × 83 inches.

Materials
(all fabric is 45 inches wide)
½ yard pale purple fabric
1 yard pale lavender fabric
1½ yards navy blue fabric
2 yards peach fabric
6 yards lavender fabric (includes backing)
quilt batting 60 × 83 inches
tracing paper
cardboard
quilt marker

Directions
Note: All measurements include a ¼-inch seam allowance. Trace patterns A, B, and C and transfer to cardboard for templates (see page 19).

Cut the following
from purple
      A (template reversed)—24
from pale lavender
      B—16
      C—16
from navy blue
      2 strips, each 3½ × 51½ inches (side borders)
      2 strips, each 3½ × 24½ inches (top and bottom borders)

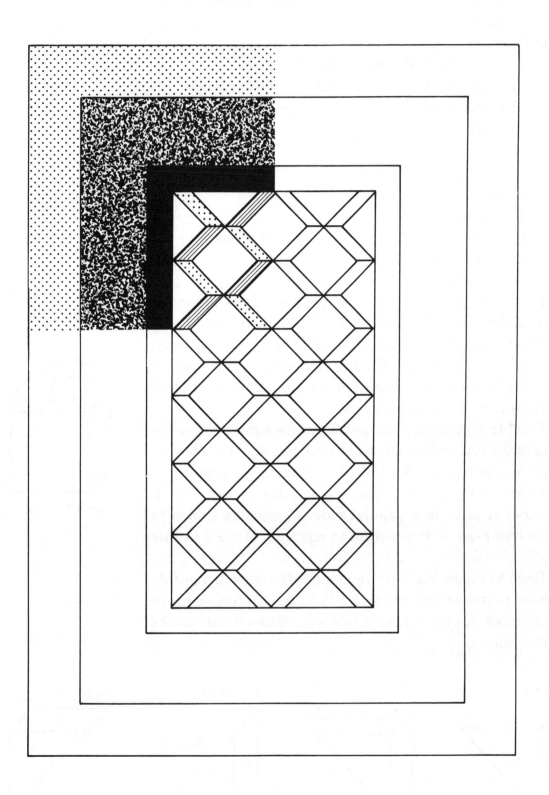

from peach

>> 2 strips, each 10½ × 71½ inches (side borders)
>> 2 strips, each 10½ × 30½ inches (top and bottom borders)

from lavender

>> 2 pieces, each 45 × 64 inches (backing)
>> 2 strips, each 6½ × 83½ inches (side borders)
>> 2 strips, each 6½ × 50½ inches (top and bottom borders
>> A—24

To make blocks

Refer to Figure 1a.

1. With right sides facing, join a lavender A piece to the left-side edge of a pale lavender B piece.

2. Press seam to one side.

3. Refer to Figure 1b. Next, join a purple A piece to the top edge of the pieced A/B unit to make block 1 as shown.

4. Press seams to one side. Make 16 of block 1 in this way.

5. Refer to Figure 2a. With right sides facing, join a lavender A piece to the side edge of a pale lavender C piece as shown. Press seam to one side.

6. Refer to Figure 2b. Next, join a purple A piece to the top edge of the A/C unit as shown to complete the half block 2. Press seams to one side. Make 6 half blocks in this way.

7. Refer to Figure 3a. With right sides facing, join a lavender A piece to a pale lavender C piece as shown to make half block 3. Press seam to one side. Make 2 in this way.

8. Refer to Figure 3b. With right sides facing, join a purple A piece to the top edge of a pale lavender C piece to make a half block 4. Press seam to one side. Make 2 half blocks in this way.

Figure 1a

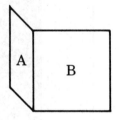

Figure 1b

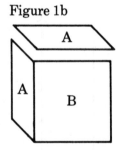

Block 1

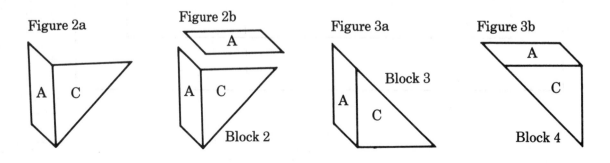

Figure 2a

Figure 2b

Block 2

Figure 3a

Block 3

Figure 3b

Block 4

154

To join blocks

Refer to Figure 4. *Note:* Blocks are set on the diagonal.

1. Arrange blocks and remaining pale lavender C pieces into 8 rows as shown.

2. With right sides facing, join the pale lavender C piece to the half block 3 in row 1. Press seam to one side.

3. Continue to join the pale lavender C pieces and the blocks in each row as shown.

4. Press seams to one side.

To join rows

Refer to Figure 5.

1. With right sides facing, join row 1 to row 2 as shown.

2. Press seam to one side.

3. Continue to join all 8 rows to make the pieced quilt top. Press seams to one side.

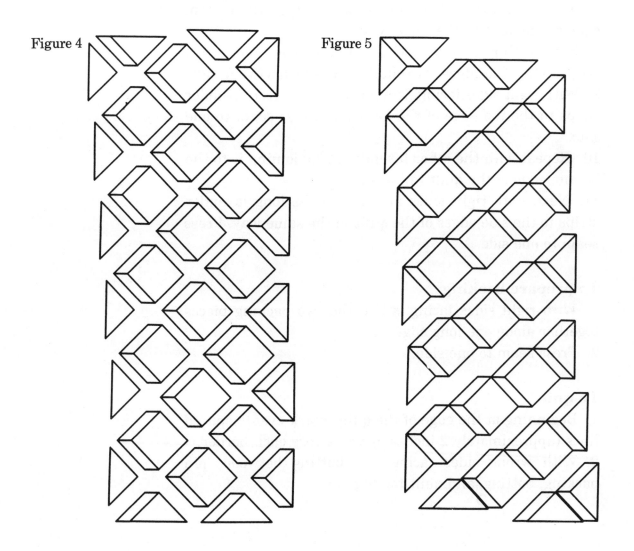

Figure 4

Figure 5

To join borders

Refer to Figure 6.

1. With right sides facing, join one of the shorter navy blue border strips to the top edge of the pieced quilt top. Press seam to one side.

2. Repeat with the remaining short navy strip on the bottom edge of the quilt.

3. Press seam to one side.

4. Next, with right sides facing, join one of the long navy blue border strips to one side edge of the quilt top. Press seam to one side.

5. Repeat with the remaining navy strip on the opposite side edge of the quilt.

6. With right sides facing, join one of the shorter peach border strips to the top edge of the quilt top. Press seam to one side.

7. Repeat with the other short peach strip on the bottom edge of the quilt in the same way.

8. Next, with right sides facing, join the remaining peach strips to the side edges of the quilt. Press seams to one side.

9. With right sides facing, join one of the shorter lavender strips to the top edge of the quilt top. Press seam to one side.

10. Repeat with the other lavender strip, joining it to the bottom edge of the quilt in the same way.

11. Next, with right sides facing, join the long lavender strips to the side edges of the quilt in the same way. Press seam to one side.

To prepare backing

1. With right sides facing, stitch the two backing pieces together along one long edge.

2. Press seam to one side.

To quilt

1. Beginning at the edge of the quilt, mark evenly spaced lines (approximately 2 inches apart) across each border.

2. With wrong sides facing and batting between, pin backing, batting, and quilt top together.

3. Beginning at the center and working outward in a sunburst pattern, take long, loose basting stitches through all three layers.

4. Using a small running stitch, quilt along all marked lines in the borders and ¼ inch from each side of all seam lines on the quilt, stopping short of the seam allowance around the outside edges.

To finish

1. When all quilting is complete, remove all basting stitches.

2. Trim batting ¼ inch smaller than the quilt top all around.

3. Trim the backing to the same size as the quilt top.

4. Turn the raw edges of the backing forward ¼ inch and press.

5. Turn the raw edges of the quilt top to the inside ¼ inch and press.

6. Pin all around and slipstitch or machine stitch all around to complete.

Figure 6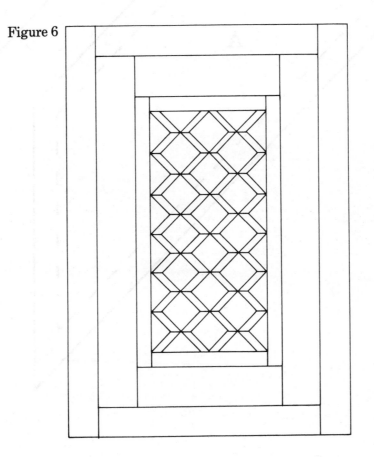

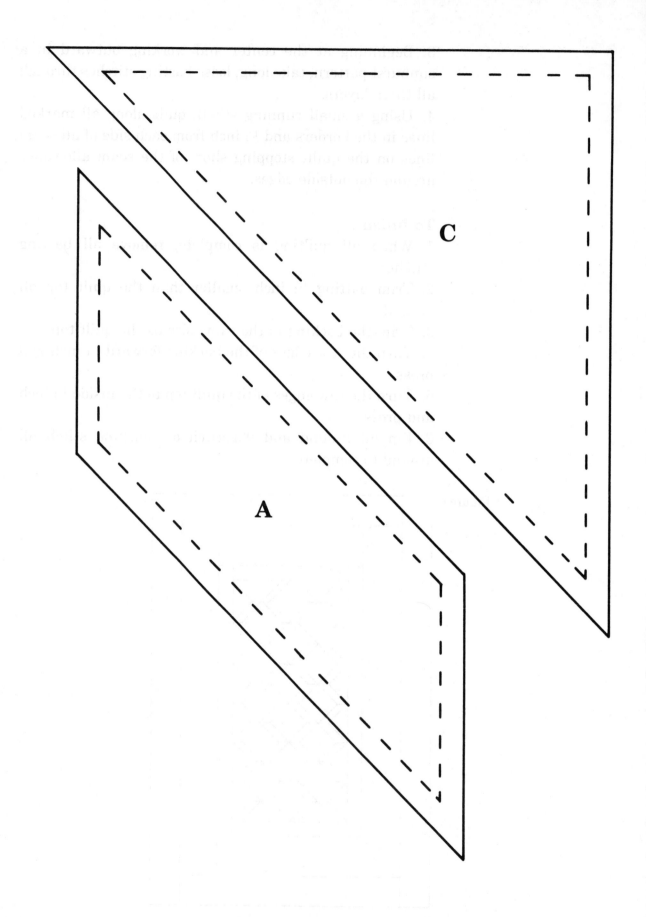

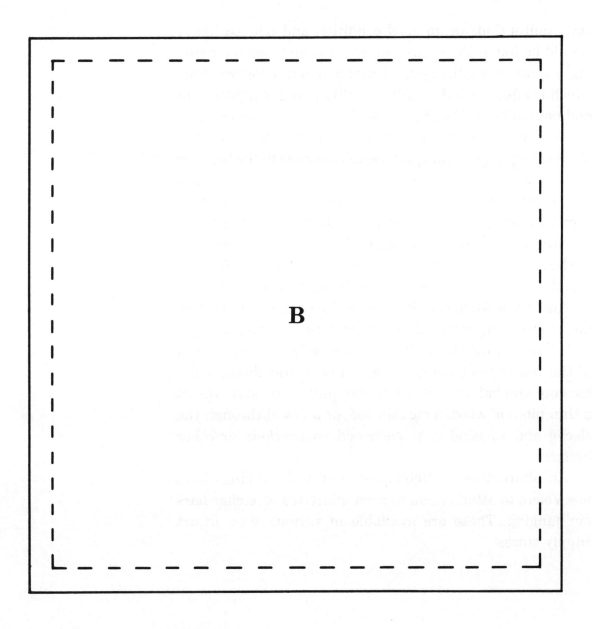

B

Hanging a Quilt

Only quilts that are in good condition and not too heavy should be hung. There are two reliable methods for hanging a quilt or wallhanging. I prefer using a Velcro strip, which is effective if the quilt or wallhanging is lightweight and not too large. For this method, machine stitch one side of the Velcro to a strip of cotton tape that is then sewn to the back top edge of the quilt. Stitch the tape to the backing fabric and batting only, not through to the quilt top, and stop short of each end. The matching side of the Velcro is then applied to a length of lath (available in lumberyards) slightly shorter than the width of the quilt. Attach the quilt to the lath and then mount on the wall. You may want to attach the bottom of the quilt in the same way.

Another method is preferable for heavier quilts. Make a fabric sleeve approximately 3½ to 4 inches deep and an inch shorter than the quilt on each end. Sew it to the back of the top edge of the quilt, again stitching through the backing and batting but not to the quilted top side. Insert a thin piece of wood, a curtain rod, or a dowel through the sleeve and suspend it at each end on brackets or other hangers.

An alternative for light quilts and wallhangings is to use Velcro to attach them to a set of artist's stretcher bars for hanging. These are available in various sizes in art supply stores.